We all make choices at ke[...]
A Spiritual Odyssey, we ca[...]
story about how to listen fo[...]
questions about the meaning of life, to live for a higher purpose, to find real and true family love — and especially how to make a difference using our unique strengths and talents.

Dr. Spurgin's journey began as young Midwestern man who met Rev. and Mrs. Moon in the late 1960's and was motivated by their "lofty venture to unify the world in a non-violent way." Hugh went on to become a highly trained scholar and management expert, build a beautiful family, and contribute real value to numerous institutions and programs, as an expression of genuine love and concern for America and the world. In a culture that seems to be losing its bearings on the most basic issues — and a world that grows more dangerous, take time to read *Passion and Grit*…You'll find plenty of wise insights that will enrich your life.

— Thomas P. McDevitt,
Chairman, The Washington Times

Dr. Hugh Spurgin's memoir is a source of inspiration that reads like the book of Acts. It is the story of a disciple, a pioneer, a builder, manager and administrator – who lives a real and full life with faith filled with passionate vision to realize goals that many consider impossible. Dr. Spurgin's story is living evidence that with God nothing is impossible.

— Franco Famularo, D.Min.
President, Universal Peace Federation, Canada
Chair, Board of Trustees, Unification Theological Seminary

Dr. Spurgin casts a warm glow on his pioneering course with Reverend and Mrs. Moon. We view a revolutionary era through the eyes of a down-to-earth, clear-headed and God-inspired man. Hugh weaves his dedication to build a new world with touching love for his wife and children. An enjoyable and informative read!

— Tyler Hendricks, Ph.D.
Former President of Unification Theology Seminary,
Former President of Family Federation for World Peace and Unification

As an early member of the Unification Church Movement in the United States, Dr Spurgin was in a position not only to contribute in major ways to its development but also to observe firsthand much of its inner workings.

Subsequently trained as a historian (earning a doctorate from Columbia University), Hugh now records much of those workings, including details of the important — and often difficult — missions he undertook and the deeply personal interactions he had with Founder Moon. This is a valuable, pioneering work capturing essential dimensions of a pioneer's life.
 — Betsy Jones, R.N., M.Ed.
 Former Vice-President, Women's Federation for World Peace, USA

Dr. Spurgin's *Passion and Grit* tells the story of a very unique *Spiritual Odyssey*, providing us with an engaging "case study" of a person of great integrity and sincerity who responds to the call of God, takes risks, and most importantly seeks to live a life of goodness that brings value to others. At a time when our world has become increasingly secularized, jaded, and even degenerate, it is refreshing to read of one man's conscientious search for God, truth and true love. As a new religious movement, the Unification Church was often caricatured and misunderstood by the media. Hugh's "spiritual odyssey" allows us to experience the birth of a new religion in a very personal and very human way, through the eyes of a believer who, with "passion and grit", contributed significantly to making the world a better place for all of us.
 — Thomas G. Walsh, Ph.D.
 Chairman, Universal Peace Federation
 President, HJ International Graduate School
 for Peace and Public Leadership

Hugh Spurgin, a graduate of the Maxwell School of Citizenship and Public Affairs at Syracuse University, Union Theological Seminary, and the Graduate School of Arts and Sciences at Columbia University, has made his marks as a research scholar, an effective educational administrator, and an inspirational teacher and leader for the Unification community and beyond. Dr. Spurgin is a visionary with an uncanny ability to connect the dots between Unification aspirations and the challenges that the world faces. He is known for honesty and candidness; his very demeanor fosters trust. These qualities and attributes are manifest in this autobiography. His important book offers deep insights into the Unification understanding of discipleship, public service, and love of country.
 — Thomas J. Ward, Ph.D.
 Provost and Professor of Peace and Development
 HJ International Graduate School for Peace and Public Leadership

PASSION AND GRIT

A SPIRITUAL ODYSSEY

HUGH SPURGIN

Copyright © 2023 by Hugh Spurgin

All rights reserved. No part of this book may be reproduced, stored in a retrieval system, or transmitted in any form or by any means—electronic, mechanical, photocopy, recording, or any other—except in the case of brief quotations embodied in critical articles and reviews, without the prior permission of the publisher.

For information:
Circles of Angels Publications
circlesofangelspublications@gmail.com

Production and creative:
jonathangullery.design@gmail.com
Cover photo by Amir Esrafili on Unsplash

FIRST EDITION

ISBN Print: 979-8-9859010-2-3
ISBN Ebook: 979-8-9859010-3-0

Printed in the United States of America

Contents

Acknowledgements	....	vii
Introduction	A Remarkable Journey	ix
Chapter 1	The Beginning	1
Chapter 2	An Extraordinary Encounter	10
Chapter 3	Commitment to a Faith Community ...	15
Chapter 4	Visit by the Founders of the Church ...	20
Chapter 5	Dangers of Communism	24
Chapter 6	Nora Enters My Life	27
Chapter 7	The Blessing	30
Chapter 8	Moving West	37
Chapter 9	Philadelphia	39
Chapter 10	One World Crusade	43
Chapter 11	Speaking Tours	49
Chapter 12	Watergate	52
Chapter 13	Madison Square Garden	54
Chapter 14	International Missionaries	58
Chapter 15	Restructuring the Church	61
Chapter 16	From Leader to Student	64

Chapter 17	Two Epic Rallies 70
Chapter 18	Higher Education 74
Chapter 19	Living in Barrytown 78
Chapter 20	Studying American History 82
Chapter 21	Our Family 84
Chapter 22	Nonprofit Missions 90
Chapter 23	Triumph and Tragedy 102
Chapter 24	Learning from a Skilled Fisherman 105
Chapter 25	Imprisonment of the Founder 110
Chapter 26	A Bold Prediction 116
Chapter 27	A Surprising Question 121
Chapter 28	Church Leadership 123
Chapter 29	Shifts in Lifestyle 129
Chapter 30	Careers of our Children 132
Chapter 31	Vice President 142
Chapter 32	Peacemaking 147
Chapter 33	Hometown 155
Chapter 34	Women for World Peace 160
Chapter 35	Moving 162
Chapter 36	A School is Born 167
Chapter 37	Government Certification 171
Chapter 38	Teenagers! 178

Chapter 39	Changing Roles	181
Chapter 40	Remembering Reverend Moon	189
Chapter 41	My Alma Mater Calls	195
Chapter 42	World Summit Conferences	202
Chapter 43	Florida	204
Chapter 44	Global Citizenship	208
Chapter 45	Into the Future	210
Addendum	... ...	212
About the Author	... ...	213

Acknowledgements

It is with deep gratitude that I acknowledge the love of my life—my amazing wife, Nora, who shared this intellectual and spiritual odyssey with me.. An author in her own right, Nora helped me immensely in writing this autobiography.

I am thankful for our four children—Andrea, Christopher, Ameri, and High—and for our three grandsons who are the gems that bring a sparkle to Nora and my lives.

My thanks to Nora and also Yeunhwa Ahmetaj, both of whom edited this autobiography, and Jonathan Gullery, who designed and prepared it for publication. I respect their professional expertise and have enjoyed working with them.

I would like to call attention to my friends who traveled this path with me. Each of them has enriched my life. I would especially like to thank colleagues who made helpful comments on my manuscript: Gordon Anderson Ph.D., Tyler Hendricks Ph.D., Michael Mickler Ph.D., Thomas Ward Ph.D., and W. Farley Jones, Esq.

INTRODUCTION

A Remarkable Journey

Life is about making decisions. It is defined by the choices we make. Indeed, a decision made as a young adult can have a profound impact on one's life. Such a course of action may lead to an incredible journey along an unanticipated path. It might even be a response to a call from God, which was my experience.

This autobiography is the story of the choices I made as a young man that launched me on a fortuitous path from a career in the civil service to leadership roles in a new religious movement founded by the charismatic Korean leader, Reverend Sun Myung Moon. I was 23 years old when I made a life-altering decision that radically changed the trajectory of my life and led to an amazing intellectual and spiritual journey to seek to help to bring about world peace.

In hindsight, I believe that God guided me from my hometown in Indiana to Washington DC—where my intellectual and spiritual quest began. It was in our nation's capital that I discovered my passion to seek to help to bring about world peace. It was there that I discovered within myself the passion, sense of responsibility, and grit to persevere through any difficulties in pursuit of that magnificent obsession.

Reverend Moon's monumental message has inspired many millions of people worldwide. As a prophet for a new age, he was responding to a call from God to usher in the kingdom of heaven on earth. He envisioned a peaceful world in which men and women would form families blessed by God. I was moved by his utopian vision of a God-centered world where people of all races, religions, and nationalities would eventually live in peace and understanding. My heart responded to such a magnanimous aspiration. My mind was enlightened by it. I was fascinated—surely, enraptured.

This memoir delineates the impact the founders of the Unification-Church, Reverend Moon and his wife, Dr. Hak Ja Han Moon have had on my life. As an early American follower, I was an eyewitness to their awe-inspiring lives and brilliant ideas. I had many firsthand, personal experiences of joy and tears with them. Through their teachings, my mind was opened to new ways of thinking about God, Jesus, humanity, science, history, the arts, and the common good.

In these pages, I have endeavored to present a glimpse of what it was like to have been an early American leader within the Unification Church movement. I have sought to provide a historical perspective on life within the church from its beginnings in the United States and to explain the dedication, self-sacrifice, and stringent discipline that were required by early members to launch a completely new religious movement.

I am grateful that I met Reverend and Mrs. Moon when I was young. Through their mentorship I became a global citizen—no longer completely limited by my cultural, religious, racial, national, or personal background. Spending time in many nations increased my understanding of the concerns of others worldwide. I have been fortunate to develop lasting friendships with people from many nations and cultures.

My commitment to the Unification Church has been steadfast. But it has not been easy to live up to the high ideals of its founders. A high level of moral conduct was expected of members. To remain faithful and active within the movement required a sense of responsibility and grit as well as passion.

The first group of Unificationists in America lived selflessly to promote the common good. I observed first-hand the commitment and perseverance of those early pioneers. They laid the foundation for the success of the movement by making personal sacrifices for a cause that is greater than themselves. As they moved from place-to-place spreading the message of the coming of a messianic age, the early followers in the USA faced strong opposition.

Drs. Sun Myung and Hak Ja Han Moon

Members who joined later are standing on the foundation laid by those early pioneers who answered God's call to participate in Reverend Moon's religious movement. They have had an easier path to travel and have been successful in large part due to the dedication and sacrifices of their predecessors.

God's providence changes and develops as it moves from one stage to another—toward the goal of a peaceful world. The Unification Church has evolved over the years. Its leaders have matured. The community of faith has expanded, broadened, and become much more diverse. As our church movement has developed, there has been a mellowing. Time has softened the sharp edges.

Unification families have settled into a more typical lifestyle. Yet, the high standards of conduct of members of our church has been amazing. While continuing to pursue the aspiration to make the world a better place, church members have sought to become good citizens in their local neighborhoods and communities.

CHAPTER 1

The Beginning

The year was 1945. In July, America's attention was drawn to Roswell, New Mexico. The first atomic bomb was tested there. Later there were reported sightings of Unidentified Flying Objects.

On May 21, 1945, there was a little-known event: Hugh and Charlotte Spurgin welcomed their first child—a baby boy. That was me! I was a "war baby," having been born three months before the end of World War II. It is a family joke that I am an alien who arrived from outer space on a UFO spaceship. Though that is not true, I was destined to play a unique role in the history of a new religious movement.

My father was from Grammer, Indiana. My mother, whose maiden name was Kesselring, was from St. Louis, Missouri. Dad served in the US Army Air Corps, which was the aerial warfare service during WWII. Initially he was stationed at Fort Leonard Wood in Missouri where dances were held to provide social activities for servicemen. He met Mom there during a Conga dance. Two years later they were married. Stationed in Roswell, Dad was unable to get a long furlough, which made a wedding in St. Louis impossible. Eager to get married, Mom boarded a bus and headed as an army bride to faraway New Mexico. She carried her wedding gown with her. Though it was a bold move, in those uncertain times, love made everything possible. For two years they lived in Roswell where they welcomed me, whom they named Hugh Dwayne

Spurgin II. After Dad's stint in the armed services, they moved to Mom's hometown of St. Louis near my maternal grandparents.

As a teenager, my father enjoyed swimming and diving. One time, when he dived into a limestone quarry that was filled with water, he hit his head on a rock. As a result, for several years severe headaches plagued him. Through spinal chiropractic adjustments, Otto Guestring (Mom's relative) was able to eliminate Dad's headaches. Impressed, he decided to become a chiropractor. The Servicemen's Readjustment Act of 1944—popularly known as the G.I. Bill—provided funds that allowed veterans to pay for college. Having benefited from chiropractic, Dad graduated from Logan Basic College of Chiropractic in St. Louis and became the first in a family of many chiropractors.

My parents and myself

At that time, chiropractic was not recognized by the leaders of the American medical establishment as a legitimate method of treatment for health problems. Since medical doctors controlled the decisions of the Indiana State Board of Health, it took several years before Dad was able to obtain a license to practice his chiropractic profession. Dad opened an office, but to his disappointment, twice the state officials closed his office. Unable to obtain a license, he went to work for Mobil Oil as a supervisor for one-half of the Mobil stations in Marion County where Indianapolis is located.

When the law was revised, he was able to pursue his chosen profession. Upon discovering that Dad had opened a part-time office, his supervisor at Mobile issued an ultimatum: "You must choose between Mobil Oil and your chiropractic practice. You cannot do both." Dad resigned. With a family of five to support, he left a secure, salaried position to follow his desire to help people with their health problems. It was a gutsy move!

Fortunately, a chiropractor in Terre Haute, Indiana who was retiring turned his practice over to my father. I was twelve years old when my parents moved to Terre Haute. I grew up with parents who believed in the natural healing of the human body and a father who gave us chiropractic adjustments for all of our ailments.

Always Conscientious

"The greatest generation" were grateful for having survived the war. Most Americans at that time were family-centered, hardworking, and patriotic. Many believed in God. My parents were all of the above and passed their moral values on to their offspring.

Being the oldest grandchild on both sides of our family probably helped to shape my character. I was always goal-oriented, responsible, and diligent. Mom said I was serious about everything. She recounted that as a child while riding a horse on a merry-go-round I focused single-mindedly on the "task at hand," acknowledging nothing else! The expectation to succeed and do well became a life pattern. I was told that when I was three years old my father taught me how to play chess and to ride a bicycle without training wheels.

My family lived in a modest home in the suburbs, and my parents had four children. My brother, Dennis, who became a chiropractor, is three years younger than I am. Three years later, my sister, Janna, joined us. When I was thirteen, my youngest sister, Gloria, was born.

With my siblings

My parents were members of Central Presbyterian Church and had a strong, loving marriage. Though they did not flaunt their beliefs, as children we inherited a strong sense of moral values and were expected to live generous and good lives. I appreciate that they passed on those values and a healthy lifestyle to us. They did not smoke, and they drank alcohol only in moderation.

We were a chiro family. My Dad, Dennis, Dennis's son, and Janna's ex-husband are chiropractors. My niece later married a chiropractor. Throughout our lives, we frequently got chiropractic adjustments in order to stay healthy. My father practiced his occupation until 1997 when he died at age seventy-six. My mother passed away in 2008 at age eighty-six.

I loved sports. As a youngster, I played baseball, basketball, golf, and swam. My father said I should not play football until my body matured, in order to avoid injury. I had a large collection of baseball cards that my Mom discarded when I went to graduate school. I might have been wealthy had she not done so! My Uncle George "Pete" Winter had box seats for the St. Louis Cardinals baseball games and periodically invited us to join him. That was exciting! We benefited from his deep pockets and generosity.

As a high school student, I played basketball, but that interest took a downturn when I was not chosen for the varsity team. I was neither tall nor talented enough. A growth spurt came later! I worked instead as the class treasurer, selling popcorn during basketball games to raise money for student activities. This was my first leadership experience. In high school, I enjoyed the opportunity to be a member of the debate team, which piqued my interest in current affairs. In addition to the normal course load, I took an advanced course in Calculus, a driving class, and a typing course that has been helpful in writing my dissertation and this autobiography.

While I was in high school and college, I had various summer jobs at a McDonald's restaurant, a Speedway gasoline station, and a factory that made Pepsi and Budweiser glass bottles. With that later company, I was a member of the glass blowers union. From the money I saved, I bought a used 1957 Chevrolet Bel Air Convertible.

Uncle Pete and Aunt Gloria (my mother's sister) owned a 2,700 acre ranch in Fenton, Missouri on the Meramec River, which included a golf course. Every summer our family and relatives spent time around campfires, riding horses, canoeing, and playing board games. After I had my own family, we continued that tradition of spending time at the ranch with my cousins and their families.

My family at the ranch

When I was a teenager Mom and Dad taught me how to play golf, yet after college I seldom played. Nonetheless, learning to play when I was young gave me a skill that was useful as a senior citizen.

At the ranch

Finding a Career

In 1963 after high school, I became a student at Indiana State University. Courses in history, political science, and world affairs piqued my interest. After taking a course in human anatomy, I decided I did not want to be a chiropractor. My joke is that I escaped from following the chiro profession. I decided to go in another direction. As a member of the debate team, I participated in tournaments on various college campuses. I was treasurer of the ISU student council and during the graduation ceremony, I received an award as the outstanding student in the social sciences.

At ISU I joined Tau Kappa Epsilon, a social fraternity. Most of the members of that TKE chapter were athletes. As a tradition, upperclassmen put the freshman (who were called "pledges") through an initiation that included hazing. My group of pledges decided to turn the tables on the upperclassmen by putting salt in the sugar bowls in the dining room. When the frat brothers discovered what we had done, all of the pledges, except for me, ran away. Because I did not hide, they praised my courage, and the football players began calling me "brass balls." For several months, that was my nickname at the fraternity. I was somewhat embarrassed by that name, yet a part of me was proud of it. It was a sign of respect that the athletes called me "brass balls," and they voted for me to be the treasurer and chaplain.

I had been planning to go to law school; however, a professor at ISU encouraged me to consider a career in public administration. In 1966, he arranged for me to do a summer internship in Cleveland, Ohio with the Cuyahoga County Mayor and Managers Association. I visited many municipalities there and published a study on the finances of all of the municipalities in that county.

I stayed in a hotel owned by Case Western Reserve University, which was two blocks from race riots in which buildings in "a ghetto" were set on fire. One morning I discovered a corpse of a man lying on the steps of the hotel and notified the manager. At night, I watched the riots from my hotel window. As a small-town boy, that big-city riot was shocking and disturbing for me.

Plans for graduate school

In 1967 after graduating magna cum laude, I enrolled in a master's degree program in public administration in the Maxwell School of Citizenship and Public Affairs at Syracuse University, which is renowned for its program in public administration. The director of the MPA program arranged for me to do a summer internship in Washington DC in the special projects office of the US Department of Navy prior to going to Syracuse. I was excited to work in our nation's capital.

My parents decided that my brother, Dennis, would benefit from spending the summer with me. Off we went to Washington where we lived in a dormitory at George Washington University. Dennis worked as a counselor at a summer camp. For two young "Hoosiers," aka, residents of Indiana, exploring the capital city was exciting and an eye-opener. When our summer ended, Dennis returned home, and I went to Syracuse. Courses in organizational psychology, administrative behavior, city planning, public policy, and public finance were my favorite subjects. I enjoyed studying at the Maxwell School and was content that I had chosen an excellent profession.

A Government Job

After graduating from Syracuse University in June 1968, I was ready for the next step. Eager to join the Peace Corps, I applied to become a city manager in Chile. Yet a prerequisite was to be fluent in Spanish. Since I had never studied that language, I was required to attend a five-week, intensive language program held in Princeton, New Jersey. Unfortunately, at the completion of the program I failed to pass the oral examination and was not accepted into the program.

Disappointed, I went to Washington DC to work as a management analyst in the special projects office of the Department of Navy where I had been employed the previous summer. That office was responsible for the administration of the Polaris/Poseidon nuclear submarine program. Because that position required a top security clearance, the U.S. government did an extensive background check on me, and I received the clearance.

I rented an apartment with two young men who were also employees of the federal government. However, that living arrangement was very short-lived when a life-changing encounter took me in a different and unexpected direction.

CHAPTER 2

An Extraordinary Encounter

I am inquisitive. As a young person, I was filled with questions about history, religion, and life itself. Raised in the Presbyterian faith, I had a typical understanding of the Christian faith, but had difficulty accepting some of the orthodox doctrines.

For me there seemed to be no adequate answer as to the reason for the existence of evil and human suffering. According to the philosopher John Stuart Mill (1806-1873), God is either wise or He is good. He cannot be both simultaneously. No one was able to explain that contradiction. I was perplexed by such an absurd dilemma.

I pondered two significant, interrelated questions: If God is omnipotent, why does He allow evil to exist? Furthermore, why do people, especially innocents, suffer? Then suddenly, I discovered a wonderful, new worldview that offered clear, comprehensive answers to those two questions and provided guidance on how to deal with the ambiguities of human life.

It was September 18, 1968. I was in a library in Washington reading about the Baha'i faith. With religion on my mind, I exited the library and was approached by Marlene Dudik (Trenbeath). She invited me to hear a lecture about God and the purpose of life. Being in the right frame of mind, I accepted the invitation and went with her and two others to hear a talk. We drove to a large Victorian house located at 1611

Upshur Street, NW. Later, I discovered it was the national headquarters of the Unified Family where a group of clean-cut, young adults were living communally. During the previous month, race riots had occurred two blocks from that location.

Philip Burley, the president of the group, explained the basic principles by which God created the universe and human beings. He declared that God wants all people to live in a state of peace and understanding and that through observing nature and human beings we can understand the Creator. Moreover, there exists an invisible spiritual world, as well as a tangible physical world. Philip indicated this was the first in a series of presentations on the Divine Principle, which I later discovered was the name that was given to the teachings of Reverend Sun Myung Moon from Korea. It is a comprehensive, systematic theology and worldview.

On the following day, Cindy Efaw gave an insightful presentation on the origin of evil and the fall of man. She revealed hidden meanings of various Biblical stories and stated that Adam and Eve were real people, not mythical figures. According to the book of Genesis, sin originated when they ate of the fruit of the tree of knowledge of good and evil. To eat the fruit was a symbol of God's precious gift of conjugal love. God intended for Adam and Eve to have a sexual relationship only after they had become mature and were ready to be blessed in marriage by God.

Regrettably, the first human ancestors disobeyed God's commandment. Due to their transgression, they were separated from God and expelled from the Garden of Eden. As a result, their descendants inherited the original sin and all of humanity has suffered the consequences of the fall. As a parent, our Heavenly Father felt deep sorrow, but maintained the original standard of conduct that was established by God. The question is why God did not prevent the fall. The answer is that He gave them free will. That explanation answered my question regarding the reasons for existence of evil and human suffering.

I was intrigued to learn that God's plan since the beginning of time had been to establish an ideal world of peace, goodness, and understanding by populating it with mature, loving couples and families.

The thought that contemporary society is not the world that the deity intended was surprising but understandable. Such a clear delineation explained the reasons for the agony and misery of human life and the need for salvation.

The next day, Nora Martin (Spurgin) gave a lecture on the life and mission of Jesus. Because the meeting rooms were being used, we sat at the kitchen table for a one-on-one presentation about Jesus. Nora indicated that Jesus was chosen by our Heavenly Father to bring humanity back to God and establish the kingdom of God on earth. A substantial physical kingdom could have come at that time, if the religious and political leaders had accepted Jesus and his message. However, due to the lack of faith of the leaders, the reign of God was postponed until the Second Coming of Christ.

Nora explained that since God gave us free will what happens depends on our response. In order for an ideal world to become a reality, humanity must follow the Messiah. The failure of leaders to recognize Jesus as the Messiah resulted in God's plan being delayed. That explanation provided an answer as to why Jesus was killed. That Jesus' crucifixion was not God's original plan was surprising, but seemed reasonable.

Due to the failure of the leaders, Jesus took an alternative course of action. He offered his life as atonement for the sins of humanity. Jesus paid the price for those who believe in him to receive spiritual salvation.

However, evil, sin, and suffering will continue until the "Son of Man" comes again to complete God's reign on earth. Jesus said, "The kingdom of heaven is like a grain of mustard seed... but when it has grown it is the greatest of shrubs and becomes a tree." (Mt 13:3) God's plan will ultimately be fulfilled.

On consecutive evenings, Sandra Singleton (Lowen) gave a series of presentations over a three day period on how God has been working to restore the human race through prophets, saints, and ultimately the Messiah. The purpose of the dispensation of the Israelites was to lay the foundation for Jesus. Similarly, the purpose of the Christian providence has been to prepare for the Second Coming of Christ.

Sandra indicated that due to past failures history repeats itself. Hence, there are parallels between what happened in the past and what is occurring now. God's providence that centered on Christianity follows a similar pattern to the development of the story of ancient Israel. We are living at a time when God has again intervened to bring His kingdom on earth.

This comprehensive historical perspective stimulated my curiosity and interest. It provided meaning to life and set me on a path to become a peacemaker. In the Divine Principle, I found an unequivocal explanation on the history of how similar events are recapitulated in order to rectify past mistakes and redeem humanity.

My primary questions were answered. Now, I needed to determine my response. Revealed by God to Reverend Moon, the Divine Principle is a set of beliefs that explain the history of God's providence. I was impressed with its universal, comprehensive, and systematic approach to major religious issues.

The Divine Principle, also called Unification theology, is filled with truths. It explains the best ways to deal with humanity's problems, by providing formidable answers to questions regarding God, Jesus, evil, history, science, and the need for salvation. The Principle explains that the ultimate goal of God is to establish a unified world of peace, i.e., "Glory to God in the highest, and on earth peace, good will toward men [and women]." (Luke 2:14) According to the Principle, God has unconditional love for all of His children. Indeed, since the beginning of time our Heavenly Father has agonized over the human chaos and suffering that was caused by the disobedience and fall of the first human ancestors.

During the Old Testament era, God gave the Ten Commandments and Mosaic Law to the Israelites. Then Jesus Christ brought love at the highest level and the gospel. Today this is a new era in human history. We live in an age of science and technology.

Many people seek fresh ideas and innovative solutions.

Young people want rational, comprehensive understandings and explanations about God, the Bible, Jesus, origins of the universe, and reasons for the chaos in the world. Indeed, that is what the teachings of Rev. Moon provide. He said that he did not come to give us age-old answers. He brought clear interpretations of passages in the Bible and new understandings of the lives and messages of the central figures in Judeo-Christian history. In my case, I wanted to know why there is human suffering and conflict, and the Divine Principle provided clear explanations.

At this point, I need to explain when and how Sun Myung Moon received his God-given mission. On Easter morning April 21, 1935, Jesus Christ appeared to the 15-year-old Sun Myung Moon while he was praying on a Korean mountainside. (Based on the Korean way of counting, he was 16.) During that encounter, Jesus told him that God had chosen him to continue the quest to build the kingdom of heaven on earth. In his autobiography, *As a Peace-Loving Global Citizen*, Rev. Moon indicated that he was hesitant initially to accept such an overwhelming responsibility, but finally, he agreed to do so, even if it meant enduring immense, personal suffering.

After reading the story of Reverend Moon's life, I considered whether the revelation that was received by such a little-known religious leader was true. For me, that possibility was an amazing, awesome thought!

CHAPTER 3

Commitment to a Faith Community

A Life-Changing Decision

Divine Principle, aka, Unification theology, is a comprehensive worldview that deals with every facet of life, including God, Jesus, human history, the natural world, the purpose of life, and the hidden meaning of passages in the Bible. It answers deep theological questions that have been debated for centuries and provides solutions to contemporary issues as well. Based on both Judeo-Christian thought and Oriental philosophy, Unification theology is a set of beliefs that explain the tenets by which God established the universe and the principles by which he will restore humanity step-by-step to the original ideal.

After hearing the presentations, I spent several weeks praying and studying a Divine Principle textbook. I pondered whether we might be living in an era when Jesus's promise of the kingdom may become a reality. I wondered, "Was the Second Coming really happening during my lifetime?" "Why now?" After contemplating the implications of the profound teachings of Reverend Moon, I considered two options: either continue to work in a secure government position, or join a small religious group with a mission to create one global family under God.

Intuitively I knew that Reverend Moon was authentic and that his revelations were true. Sensing that this is what I was being called by God to do, I decided to join this church movement with the extraordinary mission to change the world. I resolved to dedicate myself to this God-centered undertaking for this moment in history. That decision changed my life. When I said, "Yes," to God, my mind and heart were transformed, and I felt at peace. I knew that I had committed myself to testify to the messianic roles of Reverend and Mrs. Moon.

In hindsight, it has been a surprising and challenging course, which has required extraordinary faith, courage, perseverance, and self-sacrifice. Yet it was a risk I felt compelled to take! Inspired, I was excited to have discovered meaning and my mission in life—a decision that meant that I needed to resign from a secure job and start on an unpredictable adventure to make the world a better place.

It was clear that I must be willing to follow an unknown path that God had envisioned for me. As a result, I discovered my life-long obsession to seek peace on earth. In the process, I found myself playing a significant role in a modern-day, religious movement. I believe that it is likely that God had molded and prepared me for this providential mission and put a passion for world peace into my heart. Looking back, I realize that the most important events in my life happened when I had the courage to take a risk—to make a daring leap of faith into the unknown.

My covenant with God included adopting an unconventional lifestyle—living communally in a church center with a brand new group of friends. In Washington, the followers of Reverend and Mrs. Moon lived communally in three houses. They either had professional jobs or were college students. All of them tithed to the church. On weekends and evenings, they shared their faith with guests. After Reverend and Mrs. Moon moved their family to America and membership grew, most of them quit their jobs to work full-time for the church.

Believers in the Unification Church were religious, impressive, and friendly. For example, while eating dinner at the church center, once

I noticed that Nora radiated a beautiful aura—a bright white light. Nevertheless, it was the undeniable truth of the Divine Principle that captivated me, and it was the determining factor in my decision to commit myself to this great cause. My heart longed to be part of this idealistic, non-violent quest to bring about a unified world. World peace became my passion. Ever since I met the church, it became a magnificent obsession.

In November of 1968, before I met Reverend Moon in person, I accepted the proclamation that he had been commissioned by God to complete Jesus' messianic mission. I felt a divine call to join this holy community, which I did. It fulfilled my longing to live a good, honest, and meaningful life.

Since then, I have been steadfast in my dedication to the belief that a new messianic era has begun. For five decades I have endeavored to help to build an ideal, peaceful world, although it has not been without struggles or difficulties. The beliefs and lifestyle that I adopted dramatically increased my understanding of the purpose of life, but it was not easy to actualize the teachings of the Reverend Moon. Armed with the Divine Principle as my sword of truth, I sought to testify to the messianic roles of Drs. Sun Myung and Hak Ja Han Moon, the founders of our church movement. As a result, there has never been a dull moment!

God's Hope for America

Reverend Moon believed in the exceptional role that America was destined to play in God's providence. The American founding fathers created a nation in which races, nationalities, and religions would live side-by-side in a free society. America had been chosen by God with the responsibility to prepare people throughout the world for the Second Coming of Christ and the eventual establishment of the kingdom of God on earth.

With this in mind, Reverend Moon sent four missionaries from South Korea to the United States. One decade later, American missionaries went to ninety-five nations and eventually nearly every country.

Dr. Young Oon Kim

A Korean Missionary

When Dr. Young Oon Kim was a professor at Ewha Woman's University in Seoul, she became a church member. She was the first missionary sent to America by Reverend Moon. In January of 1959 Dr. Kim, whom we called, "Miss Kim," arrived in Eugene, Oregon. Having studied systematic theology in graduate school in Japan and at the University of Toronto in Canada, Dr. Kim was both spiritual and scholarly. During the 1960s, this wise, learned woman was the leader of our fledgling church in America. She was a mentor whose prayerful, enigmatic presence made a deep impression on me. Her leadership carried me successfully through my early days in the church, helping me to develop a solid foundation of faith. Her honesty and sincere dedication had a significant impact on my life and that of the early followers. It was her guidance that prepared the early pioneers for potential difficulties or persecution that they might face.

CHAPTER 4

Visit by the Founders of the Church

World Tours and a Blessing Ceremony

The founders of the Unification Church, the Drs. Sun Myung and Hak Ja Han Moon, were married in Seoul, Korea in a Blessing, aka, holy wedding ceremony, which was held at the church headquarters on April 11, 1960.

As part of their first world tour in 1965, Reverend and Mrs. Moon met in America with a small group of followers. They consecrated holy grounds in central locations in each of the forty-eight continental states and in fifty-odd nations around the world.

Their second world tour in February of 1969 brought Reverend and Mrs. Moon to Washington DC where they officiated the first marriage Blessing ceremony held outside of South Korea. That is when I first met the founders of the Unification Church. When the Moons arrived at the church headquarters they shook hands with each church member lined up in the entrance way. For the next 40 days, Reverend Moon spoke each evening about his profound personal experiences with God, whom he described as a loving Heavenly Father and us as His children.

The depth of his intimate relationship with God and his many spiritual experiences were extraordinary, spellbinding, and spoke to my soul. For me, it was clear that the life stories of the Reverend and Mrs. Moon were history-making epics of gigantic proportions that meant their followers needed to be willing to sacrifice for the sake of others, including future generations.

Members either worked on a job or went to college. I was employed by a department of the U.S. government. Very early each morning, twenty or more members gathered in the founders' living room at the headquarters of the American church in Washington DC. In such an intimate setting, we spent quality time with our founders. Such a close, personal relationship strengthened my dedication to this virtuous cause.

During that historic visit, we gathered each evening to hear lectures on the Divine Principle that were given by Hyo Won Eu, the first president of the church in South Korea. An early disciple, President Eu accompanied the Moon couple on the world tour. I was deeply moved, even enthralled, as he expounded on the teachings of the Principle. I took copious notes. His lectures strengthened my desire to learn more. In July of 1970, he passed away and continues to be revered as a great lecturer and as the author of a sacred textbook titled *Exposition of the Divine Principle*.

An American Blessing Ceremony

A core tenet of the Unification Church is that each devout couple should participate in a holy marriage ceremony in which God will anoint and bless them as a married couple, in the process freeing them from their sinful past. The doctrine of marriage and the family is the central concept in Unification thought and lifestyle. Thus, the Blessing is the primary sacrament of the church.

In this way, God's presence is destined to increase couple-by-couple worldwide. The original world God had planned was based on the family as the basic unit of society. Hence, the kingdom will be realized through communities and societies comprised of God-centered, blessed couples and families.

The purpose of the visit of Reverend and Mrs. Moon was to officiate a marriage Blessing ceremony in America, which was the first wedding held outside of South Korea. Each potential candidate was interviewed by the founders. There were six couples for whom a partner had been suggested by the Moons. When each couple accepted their matching (i.e., engagement), they descended the stairs and were met with jubilant applause. Seven couples who were previously married also participated in the ceremony. As a novice, I kept my mind focused on the lectures of President Eu and the sermons of Founder Moon—certain that I would not be a candidate for this Blessing ceremony.

The Blessing of thirteen American couples in 1969

On February 28, I watched in amazement as our church center was transformed into a venue for thirteen American couples to be blessed in marriage. But this was not an ordinary wedding. Dressed in white robes, Reverend and Mrs. Moon officiated. Sharing a common way of living, each recently married couple was entering a new stage in their lives, promising to be faithful to God and to one another. The couples who participated included an Asian/American couple and a Puerto Rican/African-American pair. This was the beginning stage in establishing a peaceful world based on interracial, intercultural, international, and God-centered marriages. That evening there was entertainment and a joyful celebration. Reverend Moon, Mrs. Moon, and each couple sang.

The next day Farley Jones became the president of the church in America, after which the Moon couple and Miss Kim departed for Europe and Japan where they officiated similar holy marriage ceremonies.

The church center settled back into a routine with a newly invigorated sense of purpose to proclaim the prophetic, timeless message of our founders, the Reverend and Mrs. Moon. On evenings and weekends, we invited guests to come to the center to hear interfaith presentations. Each of us used a different spiel to encourage people to visit the center. I spoke with people about the need to find meaning in life, and I invited guests who were interested to attend a presentation on new understandings of God, the Bible, human history, and the life and mission of Jesus.

CHAPTER 5

Dangers of Communism

My Military Service

I joined the Washington DC National Guard to fulfill my military service obligation. In March of 1969, I bid farewell, regrettably, to my faith community and began basic army training at Fort Benning, Georgia. Directly afterward, I went to Fort Gordon, Georgia for an advanced individual training program for military policemen.

Having left my close-knit, religious community, I felt alone while there. One day a Jewish friend from Brooklyn remarked, "Someday you will be famous." I wondered why he would say that in as much as he did not know much about my faith. The military milieu was in stark contrast to the holy, peace-loving community that I had left behind. During basic training, I hated being forced by a master sergeant to yell, "Kill, Kill," as I attacked a target with a bayonet.

Rather my mind and heart were focused on the spiritual warfare taking place in our world between good and evil. I realized I did not want to participate in armed combat. Returning home after six weeks, I happily rejoined my community of faith and continued to work for the next sixteen months as a budget analyst in the Manpower Administration of the US Department of Labor.

Me as a National Guardsman

America Divided

Public opinion in the United States of America was divided over America's involvement in the war in Vietnam. Left-wing activists wanted America to withdraw from the war in Vietnam. Upon my return to Washington, huge antiwar demonstrations were taking place near the White House.

As a national guardsman, I was assigned to protect the White House from demonstrators. The commanding general chose me as his bodyguard. In the general's jeep, I sat in the shotgun seat holding a loaded M16 assault rifle. Unknown to the general, I couldn't see much, since I was unable to wear my eyeglasses inside my gas mask. Thankfully, the general was safe, and I did not have to use my rifle!

The Inhumanity of Communism

Unificationists are very aware of the dangers of communism, since Rev. Moon was severely tortured by the communists in North Korea for teaching people about God.

Reverend Moon had endured intense persecution, imprisonment, torture, and unbearable physical and mental pain in four nations: Japan, North Korea, South Korea, and America. As a student activist in Japan, he was jailed and beaten. That he survived such incredible suffering throughout his adult life is amazing. He spent many decades seeking to educate people that Marxism is atheistic and materialistic—the antithesis of the world that God desires. In 1946 when Reverend Moon was in Seoul he received a revelation that he should go to North Korea to find the people of God. At that time, refugees were traveling south to escape the communist regime of Kim Il Sung. Rev. Moon, however, went north where he was imprisoned and tortured so severely that he was nearly dead and his body was thrown into an alley by the guards. His followers revived him. After recovering, he began preaching again. Again, he was arrested and incarcerated for two years and five months (1948–1950) in Heungnam prison, an infamous "death camp."

Released during the Korean War

During the Korean War, Sun Myung Moon was released by the United Nations armed forces under the command of General Douglas MacArthur. Captain Alexander Haig led the army unit that freed him from the Heungnam concentration camp. Four decades later, General Haig, who became the US Secretary of State, became Reverend Moon's neighbor and good friend.

Having experienced imprisonment and torture under a communist regime, Rev. Moon established in 1969 the Federation for Victory over Communism (VOC) movement to educate the public in a nonviolent way about the dangers of communism, which he contended was based on atheism, which is a belief that denies the existence of God.

CHAPTER 6

Nora Enters My Life

In the spring of 1970, the Reverend and Mrs. Moon announced that in October a marriage blessing ceremony would take place in South Korea. As a recent convert, I did not expect to participate. But God had another plan that radically changed my life.

Church members do not date. They practice pre-marital celibacy. A core tenet of the Unification faith is to abstain from having a romantic or sexual relationship prior to being wed. In Washington, small teams went witnessing, i.e., spreading the good news of the dawn of a new age. Frequently Nora and I were on the same team and worked well together. When Nora started a Christian fellowship program called Koinoinia, I supported her. She was an extraordinary, loving person.

In the spring of 1970, Nora moved to Kansas City, Missouri, to do church work. One day, while I was explaining to a guest the precepts in the Divine Principle, thoughts about Nora flashed through my mind, making it difficult to concentrate on the task at hand. I felt guilty about those distractions, but later I realized that God and the spiritual world had been preparing me for what was to occur later that same day. We all knew that Rev. Moon matched and married couples, but I was a novice and did not anticipate what was about to happen.

To my surprise Miss Kim, who had returned from her travels, spoke with me that evening. In a straightforward manner, she asked whether I would like to be blessed in marriage with Nora. I immediately responded "Yes," having already been prepared spiritually earlier that day. Miss Kim said she met with Nora who mentioned me as a potential partner for her.

I had been attracted to Nora, but I didn't reveal that to her or to anyone else—until Miss Kim spoke with me on that day. It was through Miss Kim that we discovered that our attraction was mutual. God is always looking out for our best interest. He used Miss Kim as a mediator who matched us. My attitude was that if I concentrate upon doing the work of God, He will find an ideal wife for me, which is precisely what happened.

My favorite photo of Nora.

When I called Nora she was hesitant, which dismayed me. Later she indicated she wanted to know how I felt before deciding herself, since she is more than six years older than I am. When I realized that her concern was the difference in our ages, I expressed my love for her and said that I definitely wanted to be blessed in marriage with her. Having heard what she wanted to hear, Nora was no longer hesitant. Together we decided that we would be happy to be blessed in marriage to one another. In that way I found a life partner. Often I have thought that it was a match that was made in heaven. Our marriage was decided by God, although we participated in that decision through our consent.

Another Life-Altering Decision

I was planning to move to Cleveland, Ohio to start a church center and had already quit my job. However, after our engagement was confirmed, Miss Kim suggested that I should move to Kansas City, in order to have a chance for Nora and me to get to know one another better and prepare spiritually to receive God's approval of our marriage.

Bearing in mind that we had to be careful not to become romantically involved until after we were blessed in marriage, Nora and I decided to pray together each evening. We got to know each other with God as our chaperone! During that summer, often we prayed on the campus of the Unity School of Christianity. It was a special place in which to meet our Heavenly Father and begin a lifelong partnership.

Miss Kim sent our photos to Reverend Moon for his perusal. In June of 1970, she reported that he had approved our matching. We were delighted. It was the beginning of a wonderful life together filled with faith, love, and respect—an eternal relationship for which I am grateful! I cherish my precious wife. She is my prized treasure.

CHAPTER 7

The Blessing

In September of 1970, Nora and I flew with three other couples to Japan before traveling to South Korea for the wedding of 777 couples. During a long flight, my heart overflowed with love for my fiancée. I was at peace and felt no anxiety about the future. I was calm and trusted that I was doing what God wanted me to do.

In Tokyo, we were greeted enthusiastically by the smiling faces of welcoming, Japanese brothers and sisters. The first night we stayed in a hotel that had a very large hot tub. Being unaccustomed to taking such hot baths, I fainted when I exited the tub. Since then, I often take hot baths in order to relax.

The Japanese church was larger and more established than our fledging group in America. The centers were populated with many single young adults who were similar in age to us. It was enriching to spend time with youth from a different culture and language. Over a span of three weeks, we visited Tokyo, Nagoya, Osaka, and an educational training center near Mt. Fuji. We conversed with devotees and learned about their activities and programs. During our visit to Tokyo, we joined Japanese speakers in inviting the public to attend an anti-communist rally to be held in Budokan Hall. We publicized that event by giving speeches ourselves from atop a minivan.

On top of a mini-van at an anti-communist rally in Tokyo.

The Blessing Ceremony

We flew from Tokyo to Seoul to be married in "The Blessing of 777 couples" on October 21, 1970. We were excited about taking part in the largest wedding ceremony that had ever been held up until that time! Since then, our church has become well-known for holding even larger mass marriage ceremonies.

Anticipating the upcoming ceremony, I felt at peace as Nora and I departed for South Korea with three other American couples. I had no hesitation about being blessed to Nora. Though I felt unworthy to receive God's grace and protection, I was happy to have found my eternal partner.

The seven American couples who were in the 777 Blessing

In South Korea, we were greeted warmly by the early followers of Reverend and Mrs. Moon. They were older and more subdued than the Japanese whom we had met. Of course, their nation was poor, having emerged from post-war destitution. The Korean people had been living under oppressive totalitarian regimes for seventy years.

Our Korean church members hosted couples from America, Europe, and Japan in what was the first international blessing ceremony officiated by our founders. We stayed in a church training center located near Seoul. In that location, several times Reverend Moon spoke to the western couples.

Also, his early disciples shared testimonies about their conversion experiences and the humble beginnings of the Korean church. Many of them had deep spiritual experiences with Jesus and Reverend Moon. Some had received revelations that at the time of the Second Coming Jesus would work through another person to complete the mission to establish the kingdom of God on earth. We eagerly absorbed their spirit-filled testimonies about the early days of the church, which provided depth to our knowledge of how God has been working at this time in history to fulfill His divine purpose.

Prior to the ceremony, Reverend Moon interviewed each potential candidate. He told Nora and me separately that we were a good match, which was in accord with our own intuition and feelings. Prior to the Blessing ceremony, all of the couples drank "holy wine" that was prepared by the leaders of the church.

During the wedding rehearsal, as we walked past the officiators, Reverend Moon whispered, "Slow down, Huge." Because I was taller than the Asian participants, I walked faster and took long strides. I appreciated that the holy officiator reminded me to slow down. Such a personal gesture in the midst of a large event indicated his concern for each person.

The 777 Blessing Ceremony

Held in a large gymnasium, the Blessing ceremony was officiated by Reverend and Mrs. Moon. The theme of the event was "World Peace through Ideal Families." Seven hundred and seventy-seven couples from ten nations participated in the event. It was exciting to share such a meaningful experience with hundreds of other couples, including our close friends from America.

The grooms wore dark suits and red ties. The brides wore traditional white Korean dresses. As Nora and I entered the stadium, the decorations and music created a wedding atmosphere. I was carrying the American flag. As a couple, we walked slowly in a line passing in front of the officiators, who were dressed in white robes and sprinkled us with holy water. We then found our designated place in front of a row of couples.

The couples in unison said "yes" to three vows. They promised to: (1) become a true man or woman who practices fidelity and lives for the sake of others; (2) become a true husband or wife who respects the True Parents' example and establishes an eternal family that brings joy to God; and (3) become a parent who educates his or her children to follow the tradition of true love for the sake of the family and world. Later, for subsequent Blessing ceremonies, a fourth vow was added: "to create an ideal family that contributes to world peace."

In a life rich in God's love, I have shared this incredible journey for fifty-three years with my remarkable, talented wife. It was exciting for Nora and me to share the precious experience of being blessed in marriage with seven hundred and seventy-six other couples. We are thankful for having received the love, trust, and grace of God through His representatives, Reverend and Mrs. Moon.

Nora and I after the wedding ceremony

Before departing, the newlywed couples from America and Europe traveled to Cheongpyeong Lake for a picnic with our founders in which Reverend Moon gave very personal advice to each couple. He predicted that Nora will bear good children.

Name of the Church

Since May of 1954 in South Korea, the official name of the Unification Church has been "The Holy Spirit Association for the Unification of World Christianity." It is a nonsectarian organization. In September of 1961, the church was legally incorporated in California under that name.

In 1970, after speaking with the church elders, W. Farley Jones (the president of the American church) decided our movement should publicly use the term Unification Church, which is synonymous with its official name as The Holy Spirit Association for the Unification of World Christianity, rather than use the Unified Family. I supported that decision, which helped to establish in the United States our identity as a legitimate church.

CHAPTER 8

Moving West

Two Become One

After having such a surreal experience in Korea, when we returned to Kansas City we were married by a magistrate. In contrast to the deeply moving religious ceremony that we had experienced in Korea the civil ceremony seemed cold and lacked meaning. Yet we recognized that it was essential that we obtain an American marriage license. We felt sorry for couples whose only experience was a secular ceremony. Both of us were virgins and prayed for 40 days before consummating our marriage. We were grateful to start our conjugal relationship centered on God.

We became the co-directors of the church center in Kansas City and moved with several members into a house near the university campus. Nora worked as a psychiatric social worker at a Veterans Administration Hospital. I had a temporary job. After work, we gave lectures on the Divine Principle to guests.

Berkeley

In January of 1971, the number of church centers was consolidated from twenty-one small centers to ten larger ones, in order to increase membership more quickly. In February, my wife and I were asked to move with our members to Berkeley, California to assist Edwin and Marie Ang, who were the co-directors of a thriving center there. Eight full-time followers moved with us. We felt that God was guiding us. We had faith that everything would be okay and were not anxious about anything.

In Berkeley near the University of California, we taught Divine Principle workshops, helped to develop educational programs, and learned much about how to run a successful center. Living near the Berkeley campus of the university during the turmoil of the 1970s, we met many college students who were seeking meaning in their lives.

At that time, America was faced with a social and moral crisis that required spiritual solutions. The youth had lost confidence in established institutions. We came in contact with the Children of God, Hare Krishna, and many new religious movements that were rampant throughout America. Most of those groups no longer exist today.

On one occasion Nora arranged for Sat Guru Maharaji, the teenage leader of the Divine Light Mission, to speak at our center, which attracted many young people. For me, as a Midwesterner with conservative leanings, it was my first exposure to "hippies" and homeless people sleeping on sidewalks.

Seven months later my wife and I became the co-directors of the church center in Philadelphia. Although we were expecting our first child in three months, faithfully we headed across the country to the city of brotherly love. We rented a stately colonial house on Overbrook Avenue, which became the Philadelphia church center. It was located near the campus of St. Joseph's University. Five church members lived with us.

CHAPTER 9

Philadelphia

Reverend Moon believed God had prepared America to play a major role at the time of the Second Coming of Christ. The United States was a place where our church movement was able to find people with open minds to support the effort to bring about one global family under God. The 1st Amendment to the U.S. Constitution guarantees the freedom of religion, speech, the press, and the right of the people peaceably to assemble and petition their government. Those basic human rights allowed our church members to evangelize openly and freely.

In December of 1971, Reverend and Mrs. Moon established their residence in America, and they were ushered on to the world stage. Reverend Moon wanted to build a solid foundation for our church movement in this wonderful and great nation. For him, America has a sacred mission to convey to people around the world the coming of a new spiritual awakening and the beginning of a new era or messianic age. He spoke publicly in order to carry that providential message directly to the American people.

Reverend Moon spoke in seven major cities on the theme, "Day of Hope." He believed that a religious awakening was coming to our nation. In February of 1972, he started a 7-city tour that began at the Lincoln Center in New York City. In each city he spoke for three consecutive evenings on the theme, "The Day of the True Family: Sun Myung Moon testifies to the New Age revealing God's plan to establish a New World." The literature advertising the event mentioned "One God, One World Religion," and "The New Messiah and You."

The Philadelphia church center

In his public addresses, Reverend Moon spoke in Korean. Initially Reverend Young Hwi Kim, the president of the church in Korea, was his interpreter. At subsequent events, Dr. Bo Hi Pak, special assistant to Reverend Moon, interpreted his speeches. As I listened to Father Moon's words, I felt proud that he was able to speak openly to the American people about God's plans.

After the arrival in America of Reverend and Mrs. Moon, church membership grew substantially. Dr. Michael Mickler, the author of *A History of the Unification Church in America, 1959-1974*, wrote: "During the years 1972-74, the Unification Church emerged as a national movement in America." Also, for the first time, many church members, including myself, affectionately began to call our founders Father Moon and Mother Moon, since that was our relationship with them.

Philadelphia was the second city on the first speaking tour. Our small center was transformed into a place of frenzied activity as we prepared for three talks in the Sheraton Philadelphia Hotel. With help from an advanced team, our staff contacted many ministers, public officials, and college students and put announcements out to the general public. On February 8, 9, and 10, the hotel ballroom was filled with inquiring minds and hearts. Although making the preparations was exhausting, seeing Reverend Moon speak publicly in the city of brotherly love to a packed ballroom filled my heart with pride and joy. After the event, we contacted people who indicated interest in receiving more information about the teachings of our founders.

I was present when Drs. Sun Myung and Hak Ja Han Moon met with Pearl S. Buck, a recipient of the Nobel Prize in Literature, in her office in Philadelphia. The daughter of American missionaries who worked in China, she was very knowledgeable about Asian culture.

A Happy Occasion!

In the midst of such activity, Andrea, our oldest child, was born in January of 1972 at Booth Memorial Birthing Center in Philadelphia—one month before the speaking tour arrived. The birthing center focused on natural childbirth. Fathers were allowed to be present during delivery. For us it was an incredible experience to welcome this little person whom we had created centered on our love for God and for one another.

Having been raised as the eldest of nine children, Nora was happy, comfortable, and capable in the delivery process and in her role as a mother. Prior to Andrea's birth, we took Lamaze childbirth classes. I was happy to be by Nora's side for the birth under the supervision of a midwife. It was a mind-blowing experience to be able to watch this miraculous life being born.

Activities in Philadelphia

I worked as a research associate at the Pennsylvania Economy League, which had offices in Philadelphia near city hall. Though my heart was with our holy community, it was essential that I support our family and church center financially.

At that time, I enrolled in a Dale Carnegie course in effective speaking and human relations that made me a more confident public speaker and helped me to develop diplomatic skills. That training program was helpful in building my confidence as a minister, teacher, and professor. Being a new father and a birthing coach gave me some interesting content for my speeches. During my career, I used the Carnegie techniques to train many lecturers and students on how to overcome the fear of speaking publicly. I taught them how to give a speech or sermon and also how to speak extemporaneously.

CHAPTER 10

One World Crusade

In December of 1972, seven One World Crusade teams were formed to do outreach to the public throughout America. I was asked to be the leader of one of those groups. Initially my team consisted of twenty members: nine from America, nine from France, one from Germany, and myself. We traveled to cities in five states in the north-central region with Minneapolis as the headquarters: Minnesota, Iowa, Nebraska, North Dakota, and South Dakota. I had never been to those states. I only knew that in the winter it was cold there! But this evangelical endeavor turned out to be a wonderful experience for Nora and me. Our team was very successful in bringing many young, new converts to our church.

In January of 1973, there was an exciting event awaiting my wife and me. Before departing for Minnesota, I stayed in Philadelphia for a few days to welcome the birth of our second child, Christopher. We were thrilled to welcome another child to our growing family. For many years, we lived in church centers in which there were no other families. The single cohorts became uncles and aunts for our children.

Myself and four state leaders in our region with Reverend Moon

I settled Nora and our baby at home, then went to Minneapolis to join my One World Crusade team. It was heart-wrenching to be separated from my beautiful family. Nora stayed in Philadelphia with our two children for a few months before coming to our Minneapolis headquarters.

In Philadelphia, I had a professional job. But I took a risky course of action. I quit my job to work for the church full-time as the director of a five-state region. We supported our team by selling candles, flowers, and other fundraising products. Leaving a good, salaried position was another decisive moment in my life. Yet I was happy to do so. With two young children, Nora was more hesitant than I was, but that decision turned out well for our family.

I felt honored to do this important mission, even though it meant giving up the security of a regular job and leaving my family behind for a while. I told the executive director of the Pennsylvania Economy League that I was quitting to work with a religious group that was founded by a Korean evangelist who I believe is the Second Coming of Christ. Startled, he stated that he is Jewish and does not believe in the first coming. But he wished me success.

Public or Personal Property?

In 1968 Nora purchased a Volkswagen, which she named "Susie." During the 1970s that little blue "Beetle" took us from the east coast to the west coast and back east. Before she left Philadelphia, the recently appointed, young leader insisted that the center needed our vehicle. Yet Nora stood steadfast in her claim to ownership, packed our children and belongings, and drove to Minnesota to join our group.

Our family in 1973

At that time, full-time members lived communally in church centers as singles. There were very few married couples like Nora and me. Much of the property was owned by the church, but not all of it. We had personal items. Yet it was sometimes a challenge for the elder blessed couples to establish a distinction between their own private property and that which belonged to the community.

At that time, we did not think about those distinctions, since we were focused on our mission. We relied on fundraising to support our work, our members, and ourselves. Our family lived in church centers. Being the only blessed couple with children who were working full-time in that region, essentially we established a standard for others to follow. Later at our workshop sites we made arrangements for childcare.

An Exciting Experience

The One World Crusade was a marvelous experience for Nora and me. I was excited to witness to young adults about Reverend Moon and his messianic message. Although it was a challenging mission, I loved leading a coterie of enthusiastic, dedicated youth. I gave many presentations on Reverend Moon's teachings, including his vision of a transnational world dedicated to the common good which is filled with love, peace, truth, justice, and goodness. Members of our crusade were committed to the cause. We traveled in 15-seat vans from state-to-state, reaching out to college students, the media, public officials, Christian ministers, and civic leaders.

We invited guests to hear lectures on Reverend Moon's teachings, held regional weekend workshops on the Divine Principle, and fundraised with flowers, candles, and grainariams. (Grainariams are flower arrangements in layered grains in a glass container). Nora used her creative talents and skills to design floral arrangements and guide others on how to make them. During the night, she would get ideas for designs, get up, and make grainariam arrangements.

In the 1960s and '70s, young American people were faced with ambiguities, a moral crisis, and distrust of institutions, which we believe required spiritual solutions. At that time, the United States was consumed with a religious and social upheaval in which thousands of young adults had created a counter-culture in which they were skeptical of conventional answers and disillusioned with traditional institutions, including long-established churches. That is the context and milieu in which many new religious movements emerged. They gained prominence during the transitional stage from an old to a new world. The Unification view has always been that it was essential to revive the traditional Judeo-Christian, moral values upon which our nation was founded, while providing simultaneously unambiguous, new answers to age-old questions.

The circumstances were right. Youth were hungry for a deeper understanding of God and the meaning of life. The north-central region was fertile ground to increase church membership by testifying to the messianic role and message of Reverend Moon. College students in our five-state region were solid, feet-on-the-ground youth with religious backgrounds. Hundreds of college students responded to the aspiration to build one global family under God. As our team traveled from campus-to-campus, our evangelical crusade took root. We found many young adults who wanted to learn more about Reverend Moon's worldview and movement. We were able to recruit students who were inspired by the vision of a peaceful world.

As the primary lecturer, I spoke forcefully about the Unification understanding of God, Jesus, the Bible, Judeo-Christian history, and most importantly about the Second Advent of Christ. Over a period of twenty-one months, more than 280 young adults became full-time members. Some dropped out of college; others quit their jobs. Most of those converts moved into a local church center and were given missions. Many of them are still in the church. However, most of them ultimately are no longer active due to the level of commitment that was required.

During a testimonial on the occasion of my 60th birthday, Dr. Thomas Ward (a member of the team) explained my enthusiasm:

> *I have had the pleasure to know Dr. Hugh Spurgin and Mrs. Nora Spurgin since 1973 when I was chosen by True Parents to be part of his IOWC [International One World Crusade] team in the North Central region. Our region included Minnesota, Iowa, North Dakota, South Dakota and Nebraska. Even though Dr. Spurgin was only in his mid-twenties at that time, he struck me as being an exceptional and very dynamic leader. He and Mrs. Spurgin lived in one small room with their children, Andrea and Christopher, and really welcomed us as a part of their family. Under the Spurgins' leadership, we had the highest witnessing results of any of the IOWC regions in the period leading up to Madison Square Garden . . .*

> *More than anything else, I remember Dr. Spurgin's fiery lectures in those early years. He had a remarkable ability to supplement the content of the Principle with his deep understanding of history and with his ineffable passion. . . . Following the completion of his Ph.D., he soon became a [corporate] officer of HSA-UWC. A public position in HSA-UWC is never easy; however, Dr. Spurgin is not the kind of person to complain about the challenges that he faces in a public position. Dr. Spurgin, congratulations to you and Nora, and thank you for your extraordinary example and accomplishments during 60 years of life.*
>
> —*Thomas J. Ward*

During the 1970s, many European followers participated in our American crusade. Nine young people from France joined my evangelical team. Several of them, including my friend Dr. Thomas Ward, were Americans who had joined the church in France.

Also, many Japanese leaders immigrated to America to help. In order to support the American movement, they led fundraising teams and established Japanese restaurants and a distribution network of wholesale fish companies.

CHAPTER 11

Speaking Tours

Every six weeks, there was a national leaders' conference usually held in New York. Listening to Reverend Moon speak, I was inspired and eager to continue the mission to bring about a spiritual revival in America. Father Moon worked tirelessly to bring hope to America. For him, the United States was in a state of decline, which required spiritual solutions. The root cause was a loss of faith in God and in traditional moral values. Rev. Moon wanted to give everyone an opportunity to participate in this God-centered dispensation and transition to a peaceful world.

The 21-City Speaking Tour

In 1973 Rev. Moon conducted a coast-to-coast, 21-city tour where he spoke for three consecutive nights in each place beginning on October 1 in Carnegie Hall in New York City. Organized protesters who were Communists and fundamentalist Christians formed outside the venue, resulting in a very raucous setting. The theme of the tour was "Christianity in Crisis: New Hope." In the second speech which was titled, "God's Hope for America," Reverend Moon asked the following rhetorical question:

> *Does it seem strange that a man from Korea is initiating an American youth movement for God? When you have a sick member*

of your family, a doctor comes from outside of your house. When your house is on fire, the firefighters come from outside. God has a strange way of fulfilling His purpose. If there is no one in America meeting your needs, there is no reason why someone from outside cannot fulfill that role. America belongs to those who love her most.

After the Carnegie Hall event, Rev. Moon gave public speeches throughout the nation accompanied by a banquet for dignitaries.

Minneapolis was one of the twenty-one cities chosen for that second Day of Hope speaking tour. We distributed many thousands of flyers and talked with thousands of college students. The turnout for the three speeches at the University of Minnesota was amazing. It exceeded our wildest expectations. On all three evenings, there were overflow crowds in a large auditorium on the university campus. We were jubilant about the opportunity for Reverend Moon to present his message of hope to enthusiastic students. After the final event, we held a victory celebration with Father and Mother Moon in a McDonald's restaurant.

Victory celebration in Minneapolis with Reverend and Mrs. Moon

In *Christianity in Crisis: New Hope; Speeches of Reverend Sun Myung Moon*, Dr. Bo Hi Pak (his translator) wrote, "We saw hundreds of college students jam-packed into the large West Bank Auditorium at the University of Minnesota, listening fervently to every word spoken."

The following year Reverend Moon conducted a 32-city speaking tour. The theme was, "The New Future of Christianity." The tour took place from February through April of 1974. It included stops in Sioux Falls, South Dakota, and Fargo, North Dakota. Reverend Moon spoke about the crisis of faith within Christianity that had led to confusion and uncertainty. He said everyone, especially Christians, must prepare themselves to receive the Second Coming of Christ. With the completion of those speeches, he had spoken in all fifty states.

CHAPTER 12

Watergate

Our nation was consumed by the Watergate crisis that engulfed the Nixon administration. While in Minneapolis, Rev. Moon arranged for full-page ads to be published in newspapers in twenty-one major cities in November of 1973 under the heading "America in Crisis: Answer to Watergate: Forgive, Love, and Unite."

In Minneapolis with the Watergate statement

Concerned about moral decline in the United States, Reverend Moon declared that it is vital that America return to God. He attributed the breakdown of the family, the rise of sexual immorality, wars, crime, racism, and mental illness to a decline in Judeo-Christian morality. He was especially concerned about the influence of Marxist thought, which denies the existence of a supreme being.

For the Watergate crisis, our members did a 40-day prayer and fasting condition, beginning on December 1, 1973, under the theme for people to "forgive, love, and unite." I was happy to participate in that effort to seek to achieve unity in our nation. On December 14, we attended the National Christmas Tree Lighting Ceremony on the ellipse. I was the leader of the public relations team. Due to the chaos surrounding the event that was a difficult task. President Richard Nixon, who was under intense pressure to resign, greeted us in Lafayette Park which is located across from the White House.

CHAPTER 13

Madison Square Garden

Even though Reverend Moon had made an effort in every state to reach out to the dignitaries, youth, and the general public, he decided in 1974 to speak in a large venue—Madison Square Garden. It was a bold move that was the first venue in an 8-city speaking tour. I could not even imagine how we would be able to fill the twenty-thousand-seat capacity of the Garden. The catchy phrase "September 18th could be your Re-Birthday" advertised the event. The title of Rev. Moon's speech was "The New Future of Christianity."

Followers gathered in New York City to campaign for this historic event. I led a team of one hundred eighty church members to campaign in NY City from August 20 until September 18, 1974 in twelve, 15-seat vans, for the upcoming speech at Madison Square Garden. Because we identified with the course of the Israelites out of bondage in Egypt, we named each van after one of the twelve tribes of ancient Israel. We lived in a hotel that was located near Columbia University at the corner of Broadway and 110th Street in the city. We canvassed and distributed tickets to the event in Harlem near the University.

The evening prior to the speech, there was a banquet attended by two hundred or more dignitaries in the ballroom of the Waldorf-Astoria Hotel. Reverend Moon and Jeannie Dixon, a well-known psychic, spoke about the coming of a new era.

Reverend Moon's speech at Madison Square Garden

The big day arrived on September 18. To an audience of twenty thousand people, Rev. Moon spoke on, "The New Future of Christianity." Madison Square Garden was overcrowded. Thousands of people were unable to enter the venue. I arranged for church members to enter the building through a back entrance. Before the speech began, I helped the security team usher a Korean protestor out of the hall.

With a stern disposition but a smile on his face, Rev. Moon proclaimed that he came to America to reveal a new revelation regarding the dawn of a new era. He issued a clarion call to action, announcing that we are living at the time of the Second Coming of Christ.

Posters inviting the public to hear the speech had been plastered everywhere. They stated that September 18 could be your "re-birthday." The night after the event, our followers removed every poster and cleaned up the streets. New Yorkers woke up to a clean city! At the

Belvedere Estate in Tarrytown, New York, the following Sunday before thousands of his followers, Rev. Moon proclaimed that the MSG speech was a victory for God. We rejoiced with the Moon family in a victory celebration.

Purchasing a Workshop Site

While I was in New York, Nora found a large three-story school building in Greenville, Iowa that we purchased for $11,000. The building had been empty for several years. When our team returned home, our staff turned it into a fabulous site. An addition had been added that included a kitchen, cafeteria, and large kindergarten room, which we used for lectures and large gatherings. $11,000 was an unbelievably low price for such a nice facility. It was a gift from God. We were able to renovate it to meet our needs.

A gathering of members in Greenville, Iowa

On weekends, supporters from the five states gathered in Greenville, Iowa to host seminars on the Divine Principle. During the week guests received advanced lectures and were trained on how to put into action the tenets of the faith. On January 1, 1975, approximately one hundred and twenty members assembled there to celebrate "God's Day", which is a holy day for the church.

At the Greenville workshop site, our children and other children of members in our region stayed with loving caregivers. My wife and I had a bedroom that served as our home base. During the week I traveled with the team. Nora often joined us. Greenville was like the internal heart of our region. It was our delight and comfort to be united each weekend with our growing children and to teach the beliefs of our church to guests.

CHAPTER 14

International Missionaries

In January of 1974 the Unification Church purchased a 250-acre estate on the Hudson River, 90 miles north of New York City in Barrytown, New York. This beautiful, bucolic setting included a 120,000-square-foot main building, two barns, and several houses. Previously it was the home of the St. Joseph's Normal Institute, a Christian Brothers' high school.

The main building on the Barrytown campus

In February of 1975 the Blessing of 1,800 couples was officiated by our founders. More than one hundred American couples participated. The theme was "World Peace through Ideal Families." Some of the Americans were wed to spouses from another nation.

In March, ninety-five Americans who had participated in this ceremony went to Barrytown to be trained to become overseas missionaries. Later that same year that venue became the campus of Unification Theological Seminary (UTS). In May after Rev. Moon spoke to these young leaders about their missions in ninety-five nations, they accepted the challenge and bravely departed for their assigned countries. Father Moon trusted them to become ambassadors for peace to nations everywhere. Those pioneers extended the global reach of our movement for world peace.

Whereas the primary responsibility of the American 777 couples was to establish a foundation for our church in the United States, the mission of the 1,800 couples was international. That was because the founders of our church movement proclaimed that the mission of America is to serve and help people everywhere.

That group of missionaries came from three former enemy nations—Japan, Germany, and America. In their adopted missionary nations they worked together, in spite of spiritual, cultural, and language differences. Cooperation among them was important for their success and a model for international, interreligious, and interracial unity among people everywhere.

Those outstanding leaders, who were newly married and had been successful trailblazers in America, took their experience and know-how overseas to lay a spiritual foundation in each of their adopted nations. Their accomplishments as missionaries were due to their sacrifices and leadership skills. Bravely they went to far-off lands, learned new languages, adapted new cultures, and endured hunger, illness, persecution, deportation, and even imprisonment. Yet they persevered and found exceptional people who had been prepared by God and the angels to respond to the message of the advent of a new age. Some new recruits in those nations had spiritual experiences that led them to contact those missionaries—who taught them about Reverend Moon and his message for humanity.

Those American missionaries were our best, most experienced leaders and lecturers. Their departure left a gigantic hole in the leadership of our American church movement. Yet true to his philosophy, Reverend Moon did not hesitate to sacrifice the well-being of our American church for the sake of the salvation of people around the globe. His view was that by serving people everywhere, America would benefit and be blessed.

Commenting on having sent those talented religious leaders overseas, speaking metaphorically, Father Moon declared, "I cut off the head and tore out the heart of our American church and sent it overseas."

The American missionaries were my co-workers and good friends. My heart was moved by their faith and courage. They endured many hardships while laying the groundwork for our movement in their adopted nations. We prayed for them knowing the difficulties that they would face and the personal sacrifices they would be required to make in order to be successful.

Those brave pioneers paved the way for an international network of peacebuilders. Later in the 1990s twelve or more nonprofit federations affiliated with the Unification Church were formed on the foundation of their work in nations everywhere. Prominent among those non-governmental organizations (NGOs) is the Universal Peace Federation, a global network of peacemakers founded by Reverend and Mrs. Moon in 2005 to promote educational and humanitarian services. Nora and I were proud to have been chosen by UPF to become Ambassadors for Peace.

CHAPTER 15

Restructuring the Church

Having sent the most experienced leaders overseas, Reverend Moon reorganized the American church. He dissolved the regional system, trained a new generation of leaders, and sent them throughout America as itinerary evangelists or as fundraisers to provide financial support.

From our north central region, more than 280 young people joined our One World Crusade and were given missions, including 40 who remained in local centers and 110 who participated in a training program for those who were chosen to become pioneer missionaries in American cities. They attended a 120-day leadership workshop held in Barrytown, New York, under Reverend Ken Sudo, an inspiring Japanese lecturer. After graduating from that program, they went out alone as trailblazers to cities throughout America. Nora was an itinerary worker (IW) who visited, guided, and nurtured many of them.

An additional 130 members in our region joined various mobile fundraising teams (MFT). A national fundraising system had been established to support the church financially by seeking donations in exchange for products such as candles and flowers.

Reverend Moon asked each regional director and Itinerary Worker, including Nora and me, to set an example by becoming pioneer evangelists. In preparation, we attended a 21-day training session with Rev. Sudo. Previously in the Minneapolis airport, Father Moon asked me whether I wanted to remain there or go to another city after finishing the training program. I requested Philadelphia, which he approved. With three members, I went to the city of brotherly love to evangelize near the campus of the University of Pennsylvania. On one occasion, I was attacked by a man who hit me on the back of my head. Nora went alone as a pioneer missionary to Waterbury, Connecticut.

With Reverend and Mrs. Moon at the airport

As an Itinerary Worker, Nora met with church pioneers in various cities in the southwest region. Later she visited trailblazers in two other geographic areas. For them, she was a mentor, confidant, advisor, and mother-figure. Nora took care of their concerns with wisdom, patience, and compassion. Trained as a psychiatric social worker, she was able to bring her counseling skills to her work as an IW.

It was a difficult time for Nora, because she placed our children (ages four and five) in a church nursery in Barrytown. Although she accepted the self-sacrifices that the mission required, it was very heart-wrenching for her to leave our two children with caregivers. Soon thereafter, happily, I became a graduate student at UTS, which was located on the Barrytown campus where the nursery was located. That enabled me to be near our children and visit them, even though I was living in a dormitory room.

CHAPTER 16

From Leader to Student

In a meeting with the regional directors, Rev. Moon mentioned that he wanted to start a seminary in order for the leaders of our church to obtain the same type of theological education that clergy from other churches receive. He indicated that was a primary reason why he came to America.

His desire was for our church leaders to become peers with Christian ministers. He wanted us to stand academically on the same level as the traditional clergy. He said that a quality theological education would enable us to communicate effectively with ministers of established churches. That required a thorough knowledge of the Scriptures and of the Judeo-Christian tradition, history, and thought.

The idyllic setting in Barrytown became the campus of the newly established Unification Theological Seminary. At the seminary, students were able to compare Unification theology with traditional Christian thought and to study many other philosophies and theologies.

Reverend Moon gave me a choice either to remain a church leader in Philadelphia or become a student at Unification Theological Seminary. I chose the latter, which required a change in my lifestyle. It meant transitioning from being a leader to being a student. For me, that was easy to do. I thrive on change and love to learn. I felt privileged and grateful to Reverend Moon for giving me and others the opportunity to become a seminary student. With an interest in the history of religion, I enjoyed my classes with excellent professors and my friendship with my fellow students.

In September of 1975, when I became a student at UTS, I was thirty. I had been a church member for seven years. I had presented the teachings of our founders to hundreds of people and had helped to organize several of Reverend Moon's speaking events. I had led church centers, evangelical crusades, and a five-state region, and I had given many sermons, lectures, and public talks.

Most important, Nora and I were raising a family. We had two beautiful children, and my heart fluttered every time they called me "Daddy." It was a life that was full and fascinating, but later I realized that God seemed to have had a long-term plan for the rest of my life.

I had learned much from being a church leader. Yet, I intuited that God had a plan for me in which I would thrive in another realm of society and find even greater happiness. Therefore, I left a "front line," evangelical mission to prepare for potential roles in the future in the realms of educational and nonprofit administration. My years as a graduate student were a reprieve from the non-stop, all-consuming evangelical activity of the previous seven years. It was a time to immerse myself in prayer, study, and conversations with professors and classmates. It was an opportunity to nurture my contemplative side and reflect on my beliefs as a church member in relationship to Christianity and other faith traditions.

Reverend David Sang Chul Kim, the second church missionary to America, was the first president of the seminary. With his colorful, energetic personality and leadership style, he guided us through those early years of setting traditions—blending together a faculty of professors from a wide variety of Christian denominations and providing us with a meaningful two years of graduate study. As students, we often joined President Kim on Sunday morning walks along a forested path in Barrytown that we called "Father's trail." Later "Mother's trail" was established.

Therese Stewart, who was a former Franciscan nun, was the Academic Dean. She brought her academic and administrative experience to her role. Dr. Young Oon Kim, whom I remembered with great respect from my early days in the church, taught courses in Unification theology and world religions. Mike Warder was Executive Vice President. Because Mike had many other major responsibilities, he seldom visited the campus nor spoke to the entire student body.

The first class of seminarians consisted of fifty-six students from nine nations. The administration, faculty, and students worked closely together to establish an outstanding, academically robust graduate school that provided a quality theological education. In his inaugural address in the chapel on September 20, 1975, Reverend Moon stated, "I strongly believe the Inaugural Convocation of the Unification Theological Seminary today is laying the cornerstone of the earthly kingdom of God." I'll never forget my pride and excitement at that historic moment in the history of the seminary. I was inspired and in high spirits.

The seminary faculty was ecumenical. They were from a variety of religious traditions: Protestant, Roman Catholic, Jewish, Eastern Orthodox, and Buddhist. Dr. Young Oon Kim was the only professor who was a member of the Unification Church. For me, study at UTS broadened my understanding of life and provided opportunities for deep discussions on significant theological topics and it provided friendship with faculty and fellow students.

I felt that the campus needed a full-time administrator. In May of 1976, I sent a message to Father Moon in which I suggested that UTS needed an administrator who lived and worked on the campus. I did not mention anyone's name. Soon thereafter, Mike Warder and his wife left the church. In September, Edwin Ang, who had joined the church in 1962, was appointed the Vice President of UTS. Dr. Ang, who had a Ph.D. in economics from the University of California at Berkeley, was patient and wise. He brought administrative, financial, and diplomatic skills to the position.

My two years at the seminary were rich and rewarding. I was honored to serve as the president of the student body. UTS provided opportunities for study, learning, prayer, meditation, intellectual development, and meaningful conversations. We had worship services every day in a beautiful chapel.

In addition to studying Unification theology, I took courses in the Bible, systematic theology, church history, philosophy, and world religions. Knowing the teachings of Reverend Moon made those studies meaningful. Although I enjoyed all of the courses, my primary interest was religious and political history.

While I was studying at UTS, Nora continued to work as an Itinerary Worker who visited our church's evangelical pioneers. Leaving the children in the Barrytown nursery was extremely hard for her to do. Yet she valiantly marched forward, carrying out her providential role and responsibilities, bringing her motherly nature, and employing her counseling skills to help the pioneers who were working alone in the mission field. Because our two lively children lived in the nursery on the Barrytown campus, I was able to spend quality time with them and with their caregivers, including Mary Soenneker Larson, who had taken care of them previously in the nursery in Greenville.

Fishing with Nets

For Reverend Moon, fishing was a time to pray, meditate, and strategize about future plans—and to teach lessons about God and life to members. Common carp were plentiful in New York in the Hudson River. In America, they were not considered to be an edible fish.

Many times Reverend Moon visited Barrytown to speak and interact with students. In the spring of 1977, he inaugurated an adventure to fish for carp in Tivoli Bay, which was connected to the Hudson River. I witnessed firsthand how he quietly guided the students and staff on how to fish using nets, giving us a precious experience with him and with one another that we will remember forever.

In order to catch carp, Rev. Moon taught us how to tie cords together to make a fishing net to put across the Tivoli Bay lagoon. On the first day of the fishing adventure, Father Moon worked quietly all day showing two Japanese students how to construct a trawl net. Initially no one else had any clue as to what was happening. Yet I was engrossed in what Father was doing as he worked late into the night. Within a few days, nearly everyone at Barrytown was helping to make the long net.

In April, more than one hundred UTS students and staff braved the freezing cold water to fish with a net five feet high and approximately 250 feet long. It was a difficult task, but we did it!

Reverend Moon taught us how to make fishing nets.

Along with book learning, our training as future leaders was designed to develop leadership skills and a sense of the importance of teamwork. We stocked a pond on the Barrytown property with the carp that we hauled from the lagoon. That seemed to be symbolic of people being transferred from this world into God's direct dominion. Jesus said to Peter and Andrew, "Follow me, and I will make you fishers of men."

(Matt 4:19) We used the net to harvest fish, which was symbolic of searching for people prepared to respond to God's new dispensation. Reverend Moon, who loved nature and enjoyed being outdoors, said we can know God through His creation.

CHAPTER 17

Two Epic Rallies

1976 was the year America celebrated its 200th anniversary as a nation. In the spring, Reverend Moon announced that he would speak publicly on June 1 at a "Bicentennial God Bless America Festival" at Yankee Stadium. On most weekdays, we were immersed in our studies at UTS. However, on each 3-day weekend in May, we campaigned in Manhattan for the big event. As the student body president, I was responsible to lead the students who worked on the campaign.

June 1, 1976 arrived. The fruits of our labors were the people who attended the event. Suddenly, a rainstorm, which was accompanied by huge gusts of wind, appeared as the program was about to begin. In disbelief, the staff covered the equipment on the stage and retrieved detached banners, posters, and flying objects. Many in the audience began singing "You are My Sunshine."

As suddenly as the storm emerged, it subsided, which allowed Rev. Moon to deliver his enlightening, timeless message. During his address, titled "God's Hope for America," he highlighted the importance of America in God's brand-new dispensation. He stated that the two primary goals for America are for people to achieve racial harmony and defeat communism ideologically:

I know God's will is to save the world. To do this, America must lead the way. This is why I came to America.... America must win, ideologically, over atheistic communism on the worldwide scale, with the unity of all races and nationalities.

Reverend Moon often said, "God is color-blind," indicating the need to achieve religious and racial reconciliation. Yet prejudices die slowly. Father Moon knew that deep-seated biases are difficult to change, but he said that they can be overcome through genuine love, since love is more powerful than hatred.

The rally at Yankee stadium

Prior to the rally, there was a 1-day program for parents of members of our church. Approximately one hundred parents attended that program and some attended the event at Yankee stadium. I was happy when my parents joined the National Parents Association. They supported my decision to become a follower of Rev. and Mrs. Moon. Not all of the parents of members were supportive of what their adult children had chosen to do with their lives.

After this event, some of us expected to return to a "normal" life, but normalcy was not in the cards! Father Moon was unrelenting in his efforts to bring his message to the American people everywhere. After Yankee Stadium, he announced that another "Bicentennial God Bless America Festival" would be held at the Washington Monument in September of 1976. In preparation, the church published an advertisement in the Washington Star under the headline "Warning to America: A Bicentennial Message."

The Washington Monument rally

Throughout the summer I was the leader for the UTS students and staff who worked on the Washington Monument campaign until the rally took place on September 18. Also as an assistant to Neil Salonen, the president of the American church, I helped to organize that historic campaign. Though Nora was expecting the birth of our third child in three months, she helped as well.

That second "Bicentennial God Bless America Festival" was held on the National Mall in Washington, a beautiful symbol of peace, freedom, and solidarity. In the shadow of the Washington Monument, Reverend Moon delivered a keynote address titled, "America and God's Will," to an estimated crowd of 300,000. In his speech, he explained America's providential mission:

> *America, transcending race and nationality, is already a model of the unified world. She must realize that the abundant Blessings, which God has been pouring upon this land, are not just for America but for the children of God throughout the world. Upon the foundation of world Christianity, America needs to exercise her responsibility as a world leader and the chosen nation of God ... Today, in this holy place, let us together lay the cornerstone of the Kingdom of God on earth. Let us all join together as the co-workers of God. Let us be the pioneers of His Kingdom.*

The following day Father Moon announced to two thousand followers that the rally was "an absolute, unconditional victory."

Announcement of a Rally in Moscow

In October of 1976, Rev. Moon declared the next rally would be a "March to Moscow," in a major effort to bring hope to the people of the Soviet Union. Fourteen years later, Reverend and Mrs. Moon met in person with the Soviet premier, Mikhail Gorbachev.

What was clear was there would be no rest for any of us. The Moon family would continue to lay a foundation for sustainable peace by working to end the Cold War between the United States and the Union of Soviet Socialist Republics.

CHAPTER 18

Higher Education

In June of 1977, graduation for the first class of seminarians took place in the chapel with fifty graduates and two hundred guests. As students we created a pathway for future classes. In his commencement address titled, "Become a Physician and Leader," Reverend Moon told us to, "go forth as God's physicians and God's leaders," to save people and create a better world.

With Dr. Herbert Richardson

Higher Education

My parents at the UTS graduation

My parents later in their lives

I graduated from our church seminary with a certificate in religious education after completing a two-year course of study. My parents attended the ceremony. I appreciate their support for what I was doing with my life. After the graduation ceremony, President Salonen asked me to go to Phoenix to help a young church leader sell a church property before continuing my graduate studies in September.

In January, Reverend Moon personally selected seven students, including myself, to receive a church scholarship with the goal for each of us to obtain a Doctor of Philosophy (Ph.D.) degree. We had a private meeting with him at the Belvedere Estate. An additional thirty students were chosen from the next three classes. It seemed as though we were being prepared for leadership roles in a variety of educational and non-profit missions.

Father Moon asked me to enroll in a graduate program in New York City in order to be near the national headquarters of the church, which I did. Soon thereafter I became the chief executive officer of two interrelated, nonprofit organizations.

Later, Father Moon asked me to study the lives and thought of the Puritans and the Pilgrim Fathers. Interested in American religious history, I agreed to do so. I was happy to follow his guidance. Like the Unification Church, the Puritans in America had a comprehensive worldview that covered every aspect of human life.

Several decades later while searching genealogy records, I discovered there were Puritans in my lineage. My ancestor, Richard Seymour, was a Puritan who fled England in 1639 and founded Norwalk, Connecticut. Richard's ancestor was the brother of Jane Seymour who married King Henry VIII of England. Who knows where research on one's lineage may lead? I believe Rev. Moon sensed that I had Puritan ancestors when he advised me what to study.

In September of 1977, I enrolled in a master of divinity program at Union Theological Seminary, which had an outstanding faculty. I studied the Bible, systematic theology, Judeo-Christian history, Christian ethics, pastoral ministry, and church polity. I took two courses with Dr.

Robert Handy, a distinguished professor of American church history. I was pleased when Professor Handy accepted my invitation to speak in Barrytown at a convocation attended by the UTS faculty and students. While at Union, I debated with several students who were advocates of liberation theology, which provides a Marxist interpretation of Christian thought. In 1979 I was awarded a Master of Divinity degree by Union Theological Seminary.

As a student at Columbia University

In September of 1979, I enrolled in a doctoral program in American history at Columbia University. In January of 1985, I was awarded a Doctor of Philosophy (Ph.D.) degree. Dr. Alden Vaughan, a scholar who specialized in the history of American Puritanism, was my mentor and thesis advisor.

CHAPTER 19

Living in Barrytown

Ameri, our third child, was born on December 16, 1976, in Northern Dutchess Hospital in Rhinebeck, New York. Rev. Moon had suggested to us the name Ameri, which is a shortened version of America. For forty days before and after the birth, we made a temporary home in a cottage on the Barrytown campus. One day, when Nora was packing to return to her mission as an Itinerary Worker, Father Moon suddenly appeared and walked directly to the crib where Ameri was sleeping. It was a lovely moment. My wife and I felt blessed to have experienced such an unexpected visit.

In January of 1978 Nora completed her three-year stint as an Itinerary Worker. Happily, we began a comforting and joyful New Year. Nora, and our long-time friend, Betsy Jones, moved into the gatehouse at Barrytown with both the Jones and Spurgin children. There, they created a home for both families and a landing spot for their student-husbands. Previously, that gatehouse had been a nursery for the children of church elders. Along with making a home for our children, Nora and Betsy served as counselors for seminary students and staff. While taking courses at Union Theological Seminary and at Columbia University, I stayed in a room in the New Yorker Hotel. On weekends, I joyfully returned to the gatehouse to spend time with my family and experience the loving warmth of our home.

The gatehouse on the Barrytown campus

One month after settling our families into the gatehouse, Reverend Moon asked Nora to be one of three International Itinerary Workers who were sent to different regions of the world. Nora traveled to South East Asia and Oceania for six weeks to mentor, comfort, and counsel missionaries who had gone to the ninety-five nations in 1975. The missionaries traveled from their assigned countries to meet with her for one week in one of five different locations: Australia, India, Hong Kong, Thailand, and Iran.

Nora was part of a three-person team that included two *Newsworld* reporters who trained those trailblazers on how to become newspaper correspondents. Counseling those missionaries made a powerful impact on Nora. Both of us deeply appreciate the work of those religious pioneers who had endured incredible hardship while laying the foundation for our movement in their adopted nations. After six weeks, Nora returned home to continue her precious role as a wife, mother, and homemaker.

Political Activity

Reverend Moon did not engage in political campaigns. Rather he sought to educate the American public about the dangers inherent in communism, which he viewed as based on an atheistic, materialistic ideology. He declared that Marxism-Leninism is a brutal form of totalitarianism that is antithetical to religion and seeks to impose total control over people's lives. Rev. Moon's horrendous treatment in a North Korean concentration camp contributed to his understanding that communism is inherently hostile to religion.

In 1980 during the American presidential campaign, a fellow student and friend of mine arranged with the chairman of the "Reagan for President Campaign" in the state of New York for several graduate students, including myself, to assist in the Reagan campaign. Though we did some door-to-door canvassing, primarily we made phone calls. I was pleased that Ronald Reagan won the election and proud to have been part of the campaign. I appreciated what President Reagan did to help to bring about the collapse of the Soviet empire.

Back Home

In 1979 after the Jones family moved to Tarrytown, NY, my wife and I shared the gatehouse with other families. In fact, twelve families lived in the same house with us at different times. Whenever a different family moved into the gatehouse the dynamics of the household were altered, especially regarding privacy. Most of the couples were comfortable with sharing some common space, as well as having their own bedrooms. However, one couple insisted on having complete privacy and a clear physical division of the house. When our children went outside to play, they would bring their two adopted children inside. Another couple wanted us to allow them and their children to have free reign of the entire house. Whenever another family moved in, adjustments were made. Each arrangement stretched our minds and hearts.

On April 12, 1979, our youngest child, High, was born in the Northern Dutchess Hospital in Rhinebeck, New York. Nora asked me if I would like to name him Hugh Dwayne Spurgin III. I did not want to do that. Rather we asked Reverend Moon to suggest a name for him. We received from Father Moon a signed paper with "High" written on it. I did not want to call him Hugh, but ironically Father Moon suggested that we name him High! It seems to me to be a lofty version of my own name! Fortunately, High likes his name.

Afterward in Barrytown, and later in New Jersey, Helen Carl from Switzerland helped to take care of our four children, while my wife and I worked full-time in Manhattan at the church headquarters.

A Wedding held at Madison Square Garden

Rev. Chung Hwan Kwak, an early disciple of Rev. Moon, was in charge of organizing the Blessing of 2,075 couples that took place in New York City at Madison Square Garden on July 1, 1982. At that time, it was the first large, mass wedding in America. It is significant that this diverse ceremony was held in the USA, the nation where people from many nations meet and blend together. With spouses from many different nations, there were many biracial, cross-cultural marriages that helped to bridge the gap between races, nations, religions, and cultures. I was amazed by Rev. Moon's efforts to break down boundaries between people from different backgrounds.

As Rev. Kwak's assistant, it was my honor to help to organize such a large, historic event. Two thousand and seventy-five couples were blessed with their family and friends attending the wedding. Many of my friends and co-workers participated in the ceremony. It was exciting to see them begin the next step in their lives. After the ceremony, those couples had a celebratory meal in the theater at MSG, which I arranged.

As the director of the Blessed Family Department, Nora counseled and nurtured many couples during the matching or engagement process. She prepared them for the ceremony at which God would bless their marriages. I should note that after Reverend Moon passed away, parents matched and prepared their children for the Blessing based on guidelines established by the church.

CHAPTER 20

Studying American History

Research and Writing!

For five years, I took graduate-level courses at Columbia University. After completing the course work, I took an oral examination testing my overall knowledge of American history. When I invited Dr. Handy to be an examiner, I did not realize there was so much tension between the faculties of Columbia and Union. The Columbia University professors spent almost as much time debating with Dr. Handy as they did questioning me, which was to my advantage. It was obvious they had very little respect for the academic standards at theological seminaries. I was happy when I passed the oral examination.

The next step was to write a doctoral dissertation based on a body of original academic research. I chose to write about Roger Williams and the English separatist tradition. Dr. Vaughan was my advisor. In 1980 I did research at the British and Harvard University Libraries.

The non-separating Congregationalists were the mainstream Puritan group that expelled Roger Williams from the Massachusetts Bay Colony. Roger Williams, a Puritan minister, was banished for advocating total separation from the Church of England. He became a founder of Rhode Island and one of the first Baptists in America. My proposition was that the beliefs of the English separatists were the primary source for Rev. Williams' theological views. Williams' doctrines were a radical application of separatist principles.

Separatist thought changed as it moved with Roger Williams across the Atlantic Ocean. There exists a significant relationship between the ecclesiological and political thought of Williams and other Baptist ministers. Williams laid the foundation for the development of the modern doctrine of separation of church and state. That was the primary conclusion of my dissertation.

In the spring 1984 I defended my dissertation, titled "Roger Williams and the Separatist Tradition: English Origins of His Religious and Political Thought," before three professors from Columbia and Dr. Handy from Union. I passed that examination and submitted the dissertation in 1984 in partial fulfillment of the requirements for the degree of Doctor of Philosophy (Ph.D.).

After an arduous nine-year process to obtain two master's degrees and a doctorate, my graduate studies came to an end. In January of 1985, I was awarded a Ph.D. degree by the Graduate School of Arts and Sciences at Columbia University. Although I enjoyed graduate school, it was a sacrifice for my family and church. I am forever indebted to Reverend Moon and the church for giving me a scholarship to attend graduate school, in order to prepare for what turned out to be a life of service within the church and in a variety of interrelated, non-profit organizations.

In 1989 my dissertation was published by the Edwin Mellen Press under the title, *Roger Williams and Puritan Radicalism in the English Separatist Tradition*.

CHAPTER 21

Our Family

Purchasing a Home

In 1983 Nora and I purchased a house in Dumont, New Jersey. Even though we had very little money, we were able to obtain a mortgage and happily settle into a four-bedroom home. That purchase enabled us to travel easily to New York City. Nora was the director of the family department of the church, guiding and counseling couples. Helen Carl helped us to take care of our four school-aged children.

On the first floor in a glassed-in porch area, I set up an office and library that was bright and cheery. I purchased my first desktop, a personal computer that I used to write my doctoral dissertation and to do work for the church and non-profit organizations. Happily, I was able to be home with my family. I spent many hours researching, studying, and writing while our children played in the adjoining living room.

We have four talented children: Andrea, Christopher, Ameri, and High. Our son, High, attended a Roman Catholic kindergarten. One Christmas, Grandma Spurgin gave Ameri and High "cabbage patch kids." They were dolls that were popular at the time, and our children treated them like their babies. Ameri loved being a "mother." High took the care of his doll "Elwood" seriously. Nora bought High a back carrier, and he walked to school every day with Elwood. One day he came home with a sad face, saying, "My teacher called Elwood a doll. I told her he was not a doll. He's my son. She made me put him on the window sill."

The other three children went to public schools. In first and second grade, Ameri made two good friends. One girl was Japanese; the other was Afghan. After a sleepover, she told us they prayed together before retiring for the night—each in her own way. We were impressed that these young girls had a sense of God working in their lives. Children are so open-hearted. We were happy that our children were comfortable with neighborhood friends from different cultural and religious backgrounds.

Our children

Our children as adults

Our children and one of the daughters-in-law

The intention of the church is to establish God-centered, blessed families as the foundation for a new world order. Yet, during the early years, the precious principle of family life was sacrificed, in order to build the ideal world as quickly as possible. My wife and I knew that it was vital to keep our children and their needs close to our hearts, to spend quality time with them, and to have memorable experiences together as a family. We were very aware that it is very important to achieve harmony between our personal and church life and sought to create a mission-life balance between devotion to our missions and love for our children. That required each of us to juggle seemingly endless responsibilities as a spouse, parent, and church leader.

In 1984 Nora and two other women were chosen to lead women's One World Crusade teams. Nora's group of seventy women moved every month from state-to-state in the mid-Atlantic region. For six months, she led the team, then returned to work in NY City at national headquarters as the director of the family department. That enabled her to live at home and commute to work. She edited and published the *Blessing Quarterly* and the *Blessed Family Journal*. An accomplished speaker and writer, Nora has always believed in the importance of excellent communication.

The Little Angels Arts School

In 1984 Rev. Moon asked me to arrange for the Unification-born second-generation children in America and Europe to study the Korean language. His request was for them to travel to Seoul at the age of twelve to attend the Sunhwa Arts School, aka, the Little Angels Arts School.

Andrea and other children departing for Korea

The Little Angels School in Korea

American students at the Little Angels School

At the Little Angels Arts School, I met with Dr. Bo Hi Pak, the chairman, and Mrs. Won Pak Choi, the principal, to make plans for a general orientation program for international students to study the Korean language. Over the years, my wife and I selected several couples to serve as dormitory parents for the western students during each school year. In September of 1984, the first group of fourteen Americans and two Europeans traveled to Korea to take language courses at the Little Angels School. Included in that initial group were our daughter, Andrea, and her future husband, Tim Porter. The following year, a second group of children, including our son Chris and Matthew Jones, the son of Farley and Betsy Jones, joined the language program.

Three years later, a third group of youth, including our daughter Ameri, and Mary Hose (Chris's future wife), attended the school. In 1991, our son High went with three Unification-born second-generation boys to study the Korean language at another school in South Korea. Like their parents, those children were trailblazers. Bravely, they embraced a different language and culture, then returned to finish high school in America.

CHAPTER 22

Nonprofit Missions

In March of 1981, while I was in graduate school, I became the chief executive officer (CEO) of two interrelated, nonprofit peace organizations that were founded during the 1970s: International Cultural Foundation (ICF) and Professors World Peace Academy (PWPA). For nearly eight years, as the secretary-general of those two nonprofits, I worked with competent staff to organize and speak at numerous academic conferences, summer seminars on Unification theology, regional seminars on pressing contemporary issues, and the International Conference on the Unity of the Sciences (ICUS), which was our premier program.

Professors World Peace Academy, International Cultural Foundation, and the International Conference on the Unity of the Sciences still exist and are active.

The International Conference on the Unity of the Sciences

The International Conference on the Unity of the Sciences was sponsored by the International Cultural Foundation. An interdisciplinary, academic forum that examines contemporary issues, ICUS began in 1972 with a few scholars and by its tenth year had expanded to a conference of more than eight hundred professors, which I helped to organize. The purpose of ICUS was to provide an annual forum for distinguished scholars from a wide range of disciplines to present academic papers on relevant topics in the natural and social sciences. PWPA became a voice for dialogue among academics on how to bring about peace among people and nations in various regions of the world.

From 1976 through 1988, I served on the staff of ICUS, including when I was in graduate school. In 1981, I became the CEO of the sponsoring organization, the International Cultural Foundation. Under the direction of the chairman and president of ICF, Reverend Kwak and President Salonen respectively, our team organized the annual ICUS event, as well as countless regional PWPA seminars.

The International Conference on the Unity of the Sciences provided a forum for dialogue among scholars in the sciences and humanities. Believing that religion and science should be complementary and work together, Reverend Moon indicated that the problems faced by the human race were primarily in the realms of spirituality and universal moral values. He challenged scientists and other scholars to explore questions about the purpose of life and to appreciate the contributions made by religion and philosophy. He emphasized the need to harmonize the spiritual and material dimensions of life.

Reverend Moon indicated academics should use multidisciplinary approaches to ameliorate the problems of society. Rev. Moon was a scientist as well as a philosopher. In Japan, he majored in electrical engineering while attending a technical engineering school affiliated with Waseda University. Rev. Moon believed that science and religion are not irreconcilable, rather he emphasized the need to synchronize those two realms.

During that time, I was instrumental in establishing Paragon House Publishers, which publishes the professional academic works of PWPA/ICUS participants and of other distinguished professors. Even though Paragon no longer publishes new volumes, it sells its existing inventory of books.

The Tenth ICUS

In America, ICUS was held each year over the four-day Thanksgiving weekend. An exception occurred in November of 1981 when the tenth ICUS was held in Seoul, South Korea where more than eight hundred distinguished scholars from more than one hundred nations attended. It was a historic, meaningful professional event.

The logistics for such a large conference was a big undertaking that required extensive planning and organization. Accommodating eight hundred participants from all over the world plus the ICUS staff was a huge operation. I met most of the professors and their spouses at the airport when they arrived, ushered them through security check points, and arranged to shuttle them to one of the six hotels that we used. At the airport, I personally greeted each scholar. Conveniently, as a foreigner, I was able to walk freely in-and-out of the security checkpoints without being hindered by the authorities who were helping us to make the airport experience pleasant for each of our guests.

Greeting professors arriving for ICUS in Korea

My primary administrative responsibilities were to handle logistics, meals, accommodations, the plenary session, and the break-out sessions for discussion of academic papers that were presented on pertinent, contemporary issues. Organizing such a gigantic conference logistically was challenging, but I was honored that I was able to participate in making arrangements for such a valuable and intellectually stimulating event with world-renowned scholars.

At the plenary session, Father Moon announced for the first time a plan to establish an international highway that would span the globe. That was a long-term, futuristic project that Mother Moon subsequently named "the Peace Road."

Tenth ICUS

It was inspiring to work with scholars on programs that highlighted the interface of religion, the natural sciences, and the social sciences. Seeking resolutions to critical problems presented opportunities for our church members to develop personal relationships with professors and share our views with them. My interactions with academics were rich and rewarding as we strove in the conference to bridge the intellectual gap between science and religion.

Global Academic Network

Professors World Peace Academy is a global network of scholars who seek to promote peace and understanding among people of all cultures, religions, races, and nations. It began in 1973 with academic seminars and dialogues between Korean and Japanese professors. Reverend Moon, the founder of PWPA, declared that the purpose of the organization was "to contribute to the solutions of urgent problems facing our modern civilization".

Reverend Moon asked Reverend Kwak and me to establish chapters of Professors World Peace Academy in seventy-two nations. Rev. Kwak was the chairman of the Board of Directors of PWPA. In the 1980s, he and I traveled to meet with groups of scholars in every region of the world, in order to organize national chapters of PWPA. We held meetings with professors from many nations at each meeting: in Peru for South America; in Costa Rica for Central America and the Caribbean islands; in Thailand for Southeast Asia; in the Philippines for Oceania and the Pacific islands; in Turkey for the Middle East; and in Ivory Coast and Kenya for Africa.

Over a period of two years, we established seventy-two national chapters with a president, vice-president, and council of advisors in each nation. They formed a global network of distinguished scholars who identified with the vision and objectives of our social religious movement.

Each PWPA chapter organized many professional seminars and programs. National chapters of PWPA sponsored seminars on issues relevant to each particular geopolitical region. In addition, throughout the 1980s, I was able to organize many scholarly meetings worldwide to mitigate historical greivance issues. In Kenya, professors met to discuss how to achieve peace between South Africa and other African nations; in Vienna, between America and the Soviet Union; in Thailand, between the Chinese and indigenous people; in Turkey, between Israelis and Palestinians; and in Peru and Costa Rica, among professors from several Latin American nations.

My visit to Ivory Coast for a PWPA meeting

Paragon House publishes the works of scientists and other scholars who attended those seminars and conferences. As I mentioned previously, Paragon House now only sells its existing books. It does not commission new works.

Several Israeli and Palestinian professors participated in a dialogue in Istanbul, even though the Palestinians were forbidden by their Arab nation-state to meet with Israelis to discuss peace in the Middle East. It was my first experience with Palestinians. Later, we held a seminar in Bethlehem, Israel in which an impressive Palestinian medical doctor spoke about the difficulties of his people. I was moved to tears by a story that he told about the difficulty of two pregnant women who struggled to reach a hospital to deliver their babies. The problem was due to a wall that had been constructed by Israel that allowed only limited access through a few check points. Even though those women could see the Israeli hospital from their homes, it took them a long time to get there. By good luck, both of them made it in time to deliver their babies in a good hospital. I am even more horrified by the murders of innocent Israelis by violent, Palestinian terrorists.

Speaking at a PWPA seminar

I attended the "Middle East Peace Initiative" (MEPI) that took place in Jerusalem, Israel from December 18—25, 2003. On December 23, approximately 20,000 people assembled in Independence Park to hear the Jerusalem Declaration for Reconciliation of the three Abrahamic faiths of Judaism, Christianity, and Islam. Clergy from those three faiths and also from the Druid religion attended the rally. I was a participant. I had no role in organizing that event, but I was proud to be an eyewitness to the history of breaking down barriers between people of "the book." The following year, Women's Federation for World Peace held a similar "Women of Peace Rally" in Jerusalem in which Nora participated.

Jerusalem rally sponsored by the Middle East Peace Initiative

During my eight years with Professors World Peace Academy, I was privileged to develop close personal relationships with many hundreds of professors from more than eighty nations. Traveling gave me a wealth of encounters with diverse peoples. I appreciated the opportunities that I had to meet with distinguished scholars, public officials, and religious leaders.

Each nation had its own unique culture and society. During an interesting episode in Kenya, I observed the life of a Maasai tribe. Originally, the Maasai were nomads, though the authorities encouraged them to live in agricultural settlements. The officials welcomed us to watch, for a fee, a ceremonial event, observing up close the Maasai culture and lifestyle.

A Journal on World Peace

My primary responsibility was to organize various ICF conferences and PWPA seminars. However, I was involved in many other programs and projects. For instance, I invited Dr. Panos Bardis, a professor at the University of Toledo and the editor of the International Social Science Review, to come to Nora and my home to discuss his proposal for PWPA to publish an international journal on world peace.

During that conversation with Panos, my son, High, who was four years of age, suddenly appeared with a sheet over his head saying, "Nobody loves me." He felt neglected because Nora and I were spending so much time with our friend. It is fortunate that Panos was very kind and said to High, "We all love you." Panos commented to Nora and me on how cute he was. Later Panos sent a very nice personal note to High. Regrettably, my wife and I were unable to spend as much time with our children when they were young as we would have liked to have done due to many church-related responsibilities.

In Virginia during a meeting of the PWPA Board of Directors, Dr. Morton A. Kaplan, President of PWPA International, and the PWPA trustees approved the journal, and asked Dr. Panos to be the editor-in-chief. Dr. Kaplan was a distinguished professor of political science at the University of Chicago.

Published for thirty-eight years, the *International Journal on World Peace* became a well-established periodical in the field of peace studies. The editorial board consisted of learned scholars from twenty-five nations, including Nobel Laureate Dr. Eugene Wigner. After Dr. Bardis passed away, Dr. Gordon L. Anderson became the editor-in-chief. Gordon has been my very good friend since he joined the church when my wife and I were in Minnesota. When I again became a church leader Gordon succeeded me as the secretary-general of PWPA and director of Paragon House Publishers. He has done an excellent job in spite of financial difficulties. I sought as often as possible to empower staff and prepare a successor for most of my missions when I departed in order to assume other responsibilities.

Academic Seminars and Published Articles

In the early 1980s, Unification Theological Seminary held advanced summer seminars on Unification theology in several locations on various topics related to the worldview of the Unification Church. Nora and I were the first church members to make presentations and publish articles on the Blessing and on Blessed marriage in the Unification Church. It was thrilling for Nora and me to do joint presentations.

At a seminar held in the Bahamas, Nora and I spoke to a group of professors of religion on "Engagement, Marriage, and Children in the Unification Church." That presentation became an article in *Lifestyle: Conversations with members of the Unification Church*, 1982, edited by Dr. Richard Quebedeaux. At a seminar in Jamaica, Nora and I spoke to a group of theologians on "Blessed Marriage in the Unification Church," published as an article in *The Family and the Unification Church*, 1983, edited by Gene G. James.

Summer Seminar on the Unification movement

Our family wearing Jamaican clothing

During the 1980s, International Cultural Foundation held introductory seminars for hundreds of scholars on Unification theology in Turkey, Kenya, Ivory Coast, Jamaica, and the Bahamas. I gave presentations on the Unification view of history, which were well-received. However, some difficult questions were raised. A distinguished Turkish public official disputed my description of the killing of 1.5 million Armenians by the Ottoman Empire as a genocide. The seminar in the Bahamas provided my wife and me with a wonderful experience in the Caribbean where we bought shirts for our children.

Though Reverend Moon was vehemently opposed to communism, he encouraged diplomacy and dialogue with public officials in the Union of Soviet Socialist Republics. He favored non-violent ways to bring about significant changes in the communist way of life and system of government in the USSR.

Dr. Morton Kaplan from University of Chicago was a renowned international relations scholar who understood the dangers of communism. In 1982 I accompanied Professor Kaplan on a trip to Vienna, Austria to meet with three prominent Soviet scholars to discuss ways in which to reconcile relations between America and the Soviet Union. Austria was a western nation that was viewed as neutral ground for that type of dialogue, since it had a special relationship with the Soviet bloc that provided a place for dialogue among academics from both nations.

Three years later, Professor Kaplan and I met in Thailand with PWPA presidents from throughout Southeast Asia. The president of a university in Bangkok explained to us that Chinese merchants dominate the economy of Thailand. From the top of a hotel, he motioned toward a Chinese man pulling a cart on the street and stated that even though that man looks rather humble, he is one of the wealthiest people in the nation. Although the Chinese in Southeast Asia usually stay out of politics, he indicated, they are often wealthy and control much of the economic activity.

CHAPTER 23

Triumph and Tragedy

Successful Rallies

In late November of 1983, the twelfth ICUS was held in Chicago. Rev. Moon gave the farewell address to an audience of eight hundred academics. The morning after the conference concluded, Father Moon asked me to arrange for the seventy-two PWPA presidents to accompany him on his speaking tour in South Korea in December, which was less than one month later.

We had only a few days in which to contact the professors from all over the world and invite them to accompany Reverend Moon on his historic tour. In reality, all of them were already on their way home. I was concerned as to whether they would be able to come to Korea on short notice, but all of them did attend. Even though this event was during the busy holiday season, it was a testament to their dedication to Reverend Moon and his peaceful message that they dropped everything to accompany him on a speaking tour in his native land.

In Korea, the seventy-two PWPA presidents traveled from city-to-city with Reverend Moon. As he spoke at Victory over Communism Rallies in eight Korean cities, their presence seemed to provide a sense of security and well-being for him and his wife. During the tour, I was responsible to lead those scholars from place-to-place. They traveled by bus to each of the eight cities. At each venue, I led them onto the stage, as the audience applauded. That provided an upbeat atmosphere for Reverend Moon's speech.

It was potentially a dangerous time for Rev. and Mrs. Moon who had received security threats. I believe that the PWPA presidents provided spiritual protection for our founders during that critical time. The fact that 72 major leaders from throughout the world were present served to protect our founders. I believe that Father and Mother Moon were safe in part due to their presence. Due to the grace of God, there were no disruptions or attempts to attack our founders.

This was a time to deepen the relationship between those distinguished professors and our staff members. It was a chance for those scholars to connect in a personal way with Rev. Moon and his vision for a peaceful world, as well as an opportunity to establish an international network of academics.

On December 18, 1983, in the middle of the tour, the first World Congress of PWPA was held in Seoul at the Little Angels School. During his speech, Reverend Moon predicted the collapse and dissolution of the Soviet Union within a period of eight years. That seemed to be impossible, but it happened in December of 1991.

Reverend and Mrs. Moon invited the PWPA presidents to their home that same evening where each of them signed a historic resolution in which they pledged to work with our founders to establish a peaceful world. My heart was overflowing with joy as I watched each of the scholars walk to the table and one-by-one sign the resolution. It was a victory—time to celebrate!

Initially Dr. Kaplan was concerned about the wording of the declaration. However, he and I were able to reach an agreement on the phraseology, and he urged all of the PWPA leaders to sign it, which they did. It was heart-warming and exciting to observe enthusiastic support from such renowned scholars for Reverend and Mrs. Moon's vision for peace. That was a triumph worthy of celebration.

Tragic News

The final rally took place on December 22 in the city of Kwangju. After the speech, Reverend and Mrs. Moon received a startling report that their seventeen-year-old son, Heung-Jin, was involved in an automobile accident in Hyde Park, New York. In fact, Heung-Jin suffered life-threatening injuries that ultimately were fatal. I will never forget the shock that I felt upon hearing the news.

After the speech, I was near Father and Mother Moon when they received that report on Heung-Jin's accident and decided to return to New York immediately. I cannot begin to imagine the pain that they as parents must have felt. On the surface, they endured the final hours of the speaking tour with stoic discipline, even though their hearts were grieving. That tragedy drew all of our members close together, as we grieved with them.

Upon their arrival in New York on December 27, I was told later that Reverend and Mrs. Moon went directly to the hospital to be at Heung-Jin's bedside. Their son was in critical condition and passed away on January 2. His parents conducted a funeral ceremony at the Belvedere Estate and proclaimed January 2 to be the "Day of Victory of Love." They prayed that the sacrifice of Heung-Jin's short life would help to bring about world peace. Nora and I attended that deeply moving and sad occasion. For the Moon family, Heung-Jin's death was offered as a spiritual condition for the benefit of humanity and for the establishment of God's kingdom on earth. Yet the loss of a beloved son understandably left a spiritual hole in the lives of the entire Moon family and all of their loyal followers.

CHAPTER 24

Learning from a Skilled Fisherman

For eight years, my mission was to educate and inform professors about the worldview of our founders and activities of our movement. We were able to establish a solid international network of scholars. However, for me that work was interspersed with a variety of activities, including fishing.

Although I had never gone deep-sea fishing, I knew that Reverend Moon loved the ocean. In his autobiography, *As a Peace-Loving Global Citizen*, he wrote that he had been a skilled fisherman since he was a young boy. While Rev. Moon was fishing, he prayed, mediated, and strategized, as he waited patiently for the fish to bite. Also, it was an opportunity for him to spend quality time with followers. On several occasions, I was in the entourage that went ocean fishing with Father Moon. Those experiences allowed me to observe him dealing with hardships and going beyond his personal limitations. He demonstrated amazing endurance and fortitude.

Often I fished in a separate boat that accompanied Father Moon's motorboat in four locations: Barrytown, NY; Gloucester, Massachusetts; Kodiak, Alaska; and Half-Moon Bay in Croton-on-the-Hudson, NY. Once, after speaking to students at Barrytown, he invited me to fish on the Hudson River with him on his motorboat. It was an opportunity to have a close, personal relationship with him. On the bow, sitting with his legs crossed, I thought that Father Moon looked like a modern-day Buddha, since he was so serene and untroubled. Indeed, I observed that he did not seem to be anxious about anything.

Reverend Moon fishing

In Massachusetts, the tuna season took place during the late summer. Reverend Moon went deep-sea fishing in Gloucester for Atlantic Bluefin Tuna; the largest ones were a thousand pounds or more. Father Moon was well-known as an avid fisherman. He taught our members to love the ocean and showed us how to develop fishing skills. He initiated the Ocean Challenge Program to train us on how to fish.

In August of 1980 and 1982, I was invited to fish in Gloucester and stayed overnight for three days at Morning Garden, which was a church property. Each morning, we got up at five o'clock and went out to sea. Landing a big Atlantic Bluefin Tuna was a huge undertaking and an event to celebrate. Raw tuna sold at very high prices in the sushi market in Japan. Amidst great excitement among the crew, Father Moon caught a gigantic 1,000 lb. tuna. Traveling in an accompanying motorboat on that day, when we returned to the shore I joined in the celebration, but was disappointed that I was unable to catch anything!

Reverend Moon with the Bluefin Tuna he caught

I had better luck deep-sea fishing with Reverend Moon's entourage in Kodiak, Alaska. In September of 1990 I was thrilled to bring in a 190 lb. Pacific halibut. A crew member helped me pull my catch into the boat. That was the biggest fish I have ever caught! The meat of that flatfish was delicious. I sent some of it home to Nora.

Once when Reverend Moon traveled north in the Bering Sea toward the Arctic Ocean, I was in an accompanying boat. During a turbulent storm with very high waves, our boats rocked wildly in the choppy sea, but I observed that Father Moon remained very calm. In the midst of a storm, I observed that he was at peace and very brave. He continued unfazed by the ferocity of the storm. Needless to say, I was relieved to get back on solid ground!

On another occasion in 1991, standing on a river bank in Kodiak, I went salmon fishing and had limited success. That was when I watched Father Moon catch a 25 lb. King Salmon.

The Pacific halibut that I caught in Alaska

For several decades in the spring, Reverend Moon fished for striped bass in the Hudson River after delivering a sermon at Belvedere. He fished in a boat that was docked at Half Moon Bay in Croton, NY, which is located near the East Garden Estate. On several occasions in

1990 and 1991, I was in a boat that accompanied his motorboat. I caught a few striped bass, but I never caught a large one. In the 1990s, Nora had several chances to fish with Father Moon in Alaska and on the Hudson River after she became president of WFWP, USA. On one occasion on the Hudson River, Father Moon immediately noticed that she had caught a very large striped bass. That Nora had caught such a large fish was for Father Moon a sign of the future success of WFWP in America. For him, like for Jesus, catching fish was symbolic of ushering people into God's dominion.

Rev. Moon—the fisherman

CHAPTER 25

Imprisonment of the Founder

Kidnappings

Reverend Moon stirred up controversy in America and our church faced strong opposition. Fear, hysteria, animosity, false accusations, and sensationalistic journalism resulted in persecution. Church members were vilified as "moonies." The Cult Awareness Network (CAN) was an organization in which anti-cultists kidnapped members of new religions, confined them, and subjected them to coercion. As faith-breakers, they used intimidation and physical force to get young adults to renounce their membership in their newfound faith. Subsequently, they kidnapped and used force against new converts to our church. Hired by parents for a sizable fee, Ted Patrick and other thugs promised parents that they could "deprogram" their adult children. Those deprogrammers used violence to get those young adults to renounce their newfound faith.

It was a horrific experience for those young adults who were forcefully incarcerated and subjected to intimidation and harassment. In the case of Unification Church members, some of them pretended to recant in order to get away. Others left the church. Fortunately, many of them escaped, and most of them rejoined the church.

Young adults who were new converts had voluntarily joined our church. Most of them were very intelligent, compassionate, and emotionally stable. In 1978 I wrote an essay in which I explained that a genuine religious conversion experience is not brainwashing. These young people had undergone a traditional conversion experience. In 1996 CAN lost a major lawsuit and filed for bankruptcy.

The Persecution and Prosecution of Reverend Moon

During his lifetime, Reverend Moon was imprisoned six times in four nations: Japan, North Korea, South Korea, and America. He survived two years and eight months in a notorious North Korean labor camp, due to his faith in God.

In America, I witnessed firsthand the character assassination, false accusations, and persecution of Reverend Moon that was inflamed by a biased, commercial media and public officials who stoked that fear. Threatened by his message to change the world, Reverend Moon's opponents were eager to find a reason to sabotage his religious work and see Rev. Moon leave America. In 1991 Carlton Sherwood, a Pulitzer Prize author, published *Inquisition: The Persecution and Prosecution of Rev. Sun Myung Moon*. His book explained in detail the religious bigotry that surrounded the trumped-up case against Reverend Moon.

In such a hostile milieu, in October of 1981 Reverend Moon was arraigned on charges of tax evasion in the Federal Court in New York for failing to pay $7,000 in taxes on interest that had accumulated in a church bank account. After his arraignment, he spoke to a crowd gathered outside the courthouse at Foley Square, declaring that his case was due to racial and religious discrimination. Aware that he was controversial, Rev. Moon did not shy away from the persecution and prosecution that ensued.

In his testimony before the Subcommittee on the Constitution of the Committee on the Judiciary of the US Senate, Reverend Moon declared on June 26, 1984:

> *In the providence of God, the case of Reverend Moon has become a rally point for religious freedom in the United States. I stand convicted for no other reason than my religious beliefs and practices. I am to be punished for being who I am. This has shocked and awakened the conscience of America. Many religious leaders and believers of all faiths have stood up in outrage. They are registering their protests. Most important of all, they are united. Their unity will insure the survival of America....*
>
> *The issue today is the very survival of America and the free world. To assure this survival, I am willing to suffer any indignity, to go any distance, to do any labor, and to bear any cross. I am even willing to give my life, if that will ensure that the nation would survive and I am able to do God's will.*

Rev. Moon had been in Korea when he was indicted. At that time, the United States did not have an extradition treaty with South Korea. Although American officials could not compel him to return to America, Rev. Moon decided to return voluntarily to stand trial. Observing this with my own eyes, I noted his courage and willingness to face prosecution if necessary, in order to save our nation from moral decline.

Unjustly Imprisoned

The U.S. government claimed that church funds had been used by Rev. Moon for his personal benefit. Because of the controversy, the attorneys for Rev. Moon wanted a non-jury trial before a judge, a proposal that was rejected. Hence, in the case of *The United States of America vs. Rev. Sun Myung Moon*, in May of 1982 the jury returned a verdict of guilty of tax evasion. Two months later, Rev. Moon was sentenced to eighteen months in prison and was fined $25,000. The Supreme Court decided not to hear his appeal.

Religious Liberty

A "Rally for Religious Freedom" was held, proclaiming the threat to religious liberty that was posed by the imprisonment of Reverend Moon. Five hundred clergy gathered at an event that was held in Washington's Capitol Hill Hyatt Hotel. One month later, Rev. Moon testified on the importance of religious liberty at a meeting of the U.S. Senate Judiciary Subcommittee on the Constitution. US Senator Orrin Hatch chaired that hearing. A while later, Rev. Moon spoke at a VIP Senate Banquet held in the Dirksen Senate Office Building.

Before Reverend Moon was imprisoned

On July 19, 1984, the day before Father Moon departed for Danbury prison, he spoke for many hours at the East Garden Estate to a handful of church leaders. As I sat at his feet in the small, yellow room, I could feel Father Moon's resolve to accept this unjust sentence and use it to further the progress of his mission to save America. I believed that the verdict was a tragic mistake by America. I found it incredulous that Rev. Moon would be persecuted in our nation where the right to freedom of religion is guaranteed by the U.S. Constitution.

Very late that night after Rev. Moon finished speaking, he asked those who were present to pray on the grounds of the East Garden Estate. I did. Regrettably at some point I dozed off. When I discovered later that Father and Mother Moon and their son, Hyo-Jin, had stayed awake all night praying, I felt very deep regret for my failure to continue to pray unceasingly throughout the night.

The following evening, Father Moon delivered a farewell message at the East Garden Estate to a much larger group. At 10 p.m., he departed for the Federal Correctional Institution in Danbury, Connecticut. I found it hard to believe that this was happening in America. I will never forget my sorrow and anguish as he departed. I sensed that this was an effort by the authorities to inhibit his freedom to deliver his providential views directly to the American people. His powerful message was a threat to the status quo, aka, to the elite establishment.

Reverend Moon in Danbury prison

Reverend Moon never complained. He blamed no one for his imprisonment. Rather than abandon his providential mission, he was willing to be incarcerated in a Federal penitentiary. From my perspective, he went to prison in order to revive the Judeo-Christian tradition in our nation. He earned the respect of fellow inmates who reported that he had been a model prisoner. With President Reagan's approval, Rev. Moon was released temporarily to attend God's Day, which is a church holy day that was celebrated at that time on January 1st.

As a result of Rev. Moon's unjust imprisonment, many Christian clergy affirmed his innocence. They realized that his case set a precedent for the religious persecution of people of all faiths. Prior to 1984 Rev. Moon was treated by well-known ministers as a pariah. After his incarceration, rallies for religious freedom were held featuring speeches from prominent ministers. He turned his imprisonment into a success story, proclaiming that religious liberty is at the foundation for all civil rights and freedoms in America.

Widely known ministers, public officials, and civic organizations filed amici curiae (i.e., friend-of-the-court) briefs with the US Supreme Court in support of Rev. Moon's appeal. Those filing briefs included prominent leaders such as Reverend Jerry Falwell (chairman of the Moral Majority), Reverend Joseph Lowry (chairman of Southern Christian Leadership Conference), Dr. Laurence Tribe (constitutional scholar at Harvard University), Orrin Hatch (US Senator), and Eugene McCarthy (US Senator and presidential candidate).

Established churches and institutions that filed friend-of-the-court briefs included The America Civil Liberties Union, The National Council of Churches of Christ in the USA, American Baptist Churches in the USA, The Presbyterian Church (USA), The Catholic League for Religious and Civil Rights, The Coalition of Catholic Laymen, The Southern Christian Leadership Conference, The Association of Evangelicals, and The Church of Jesus Christ of Latter-Day Saints.

Though they may have disagreed with Reverend Moon's theology, each leader and organization stressed the importance of protecting freedom of religion as guaranteed by the U.S. Constitution. Yet, disturbingly, the U.S. Supreme Court refused to consider the appeal.

CHAPTER 26

A Bold Prediction

While in prison, Reverend Moon made some bold decisions regarding future institutions and projects. He established *The Washington Times* newspaper. *The Times* has had a major impact in the media world. For instance, it was delivered daily to the White House for President Ronald Reagan and others to read. Rev. Moon also founded twelve related peace-making organizations in various segments of society. I helped to manage the operations and staff of several of the non-profit organizations.

Numerous projects were initiated while Rev. Moon was incarcerated in Danbury prison, including a conference in August of 1985 on "The Fall of the Soviet Empire." Dr. Morton Kaplan from the University of Chicago was president of PWPA International and chairman of several ICUS conferences. I worked closely with him in organizing many conferences and programs.

In September of 1984 during a visit with Reverend Moon in Danbury prison, Professor Kaplan proposed that the second International Congress of PWPA be held in Switzerland on the decline of the Soviet Union, the nation that was the flagship of communism. Reverend Moon accepted his recommendation but made a bold request to name the conference: "The Fall of the Soviet Empire." Our founder was steadfast in his desire that the title of the conference be a declaration, rather than be ambiguous in its meaning. Later Dr. Kaplan told me that he was hesitant to make such a bold declarative statement for an academic conference, but that he finally decided to accept Reverend Moon's request.

The title was brilliant and prophetic. Reverend Moon was on the mark! I heard him declare several times that the Soviet Empire would fall within seventy years of its founding. In fact, as he had predicted, the Union of Soviet Socialist Republics (USSR) collapsed in December of 1991, which was six years after the PWPA conference took place.

The PWPA conference held in Geneva

Reverend Moon asked me to organize that conference on "The Fall of the Soviet Empire." As the chairman of PWPA, Rev. Kwak was my immediate supervisor. The program was held for four days from August 13-17, 1985 in the Inter-Continental Hotel in Geneva, Switzerland, which was across the street from the Soviet embassy.

Dr. Kaplan chose Professor Alexander Shtromas to contact renowned Sovietologists worldwide to make presentations. Alex Shtromas, who was from Lithuania, was a legal scholar who had been trained at the

University of Moscow. He taught at the University of Bradford in England, the University of Chicago, Boston College, Hillsdale College, and the Hoover Institution.

More than eighty academic papers were presented by distinguished professors on the demise and dissolution of the Soviet Union, even though the vast majority of Sovietologists contended that the USSR would never ever collapse. Playing a significant role in such a world-changing event is something I will always cherish. I was proud to be on the cutting edge of helping those who were instrumental in bringing about the downfall of the Soviet empire, which freed millions of people from the shackles of communist governments.

Interfaith Activities

Even though he was incarcerated, Founder Moon continued to lead our church movement and encourage his followers to reach out to influential leaders. He encouraged our members to meet with Christian clergy. I personally attended worship services in many different churches and participated in numerous interdenominational programs, which were often breakfast meetings.

In October of 1983 for forty days, I went to Toledo, Ohio where I met privately with many ministers and later with their congregations. I explained the dangers of communism to them. CAUSA is a 501(c)(3) not-for-profit corporation that was established with the mission to inform the public through educational seminars about the threat of communist governments. The leaders of CAUSA developed an ideological critique and counterproposal to communism. I used the content from that CAUSA manual to explain to the ministers that Marxist thought is atheistic and a fundamental threat to the survival of the democratic way of life.

Even though Reverend Moon believed in the central role of Christianity in world history, he implored us also to dialogue with leaders of all of the major world religions. In November of 1985, "The Assembly of the World's Religions" conference took place for five days in McAfee,

New Jersey with more than six hundred participants. I observed with admiration as renowned Christian ministers, Jewish rabbis, Muslim imams, and Buddhist monks spoke and participated in a ceremony signifying their desire to transcend national, racial, and religious barriers. It was a moving experience for everyone. At the farewell banquet, our founder emphasized the need for cooperation and unity among the leaders of religious organizations.

In 1986 in Mobile, Alabama, the Institute of Biblical Studies held a graduation ceremony. Two of the graduates were my good friends and colleagues, Rev. Paul Werner and Rev. Martin Porter. Each of them was awarded a doctorate in Biblical studies. I was honored to give the commencement address.

Speaking at the graduation ceremony in Alabama

Federations for World Peace

The Unification Church adopted the name, Family Federation for World Peace and Unification (FFWPU) in the period from 1996 to 1997, but kept the official, legal name, which is the Holy Spirit Association for the Unification of World Christianity. Those two organizations, i.e., FFWPU and HSA-UWC, are synonymous.

Father and Mother Moon were very creative and innovative. As God's providence developed, there were many new beginnings. Our religious movement has always been in a constant state of flux or change. During the 1990s, more than a dozen interrelated, peace federations were founded. Each transnational organization had a unique mission and constituency. Most of the participants in those federations were not members of the Unification Church per se.

CHAPTER 27

A Surprising Question

Reverend Moon was incarcerated for thirteen months, including the time he spent in the Phoenix Halfway House in Brooklyn. Upon his release on August 20, 1985, he spoke in Washington DC at the "God and Freedom Banquet to Welcome Reverend Sun Myung Moon on His Release from Prison." Fifteen hundred clergy and dignitaries, including several very prominent Christian ministers, participated.

Before departing for the nation's capital, Rev. Moon had breakfast at the East Garden Estate. Unlike other times, he was in a hurry. Only two Koreans and I were present. Later, I learned that many of the church leaders were in Washington DC, since Rev. Moon was going to the nation's capital to speak at a welcome home banquet.

Suddenly in English, Rev. Moon asked me, "Do you love or fear me?" Startled, I answered, "Both." Then he asked that identical question again. I responded, "I love you," realizing that I should have expressed my love for him more explicitly the first time. As Father Moon rose from the table, he asked me that question a third time. Emphatically I declared, "I love you," as he departed from the room. I was stunned. "Why did he ask that same question three times?"

I have not mentioned to anyone, except for Nora, anything about that deeply personal experience. Yet I will never forget what happened that morning in 1985. It is a cherished memory that will be with me forever.

That experience brought to mind a flashback regarding another experience that I had with Father Moon thirteen months prior to that date. On July 19, 1984, the night before Father Moon was scheduled to depart for Danbury prison the next evening, he asked a few of us to pray on the grounds of the East Garden Estate. I prayed fervently and unceasingly, but unfortunately at some point during the night I dozed off. Afterward, I felt sorrow and guilt that I had not stayed completely awake the entire night and regret about my failure to do so at that critical moment in God's providence.

At that time, I could not help but be reminded of the failures of Peter and the other two disciples to stay awake in Gethsemane prior to Jesus' arrest. However, I did not want to consider the implications of that similarity. I did have a sense at that moment that Father Moon had forgiven me for my earlier failure and had given me another chance to prove my commitment, loyalty, and love for him.

redemption of humanity. At that historic rock, some ministers testified that they had spiritual experiences in which Jesus and/or the Holy Spirit appeared to them.

Two large-scale projects stand out: In February of 1985 our headquarters sent a packet to three hundred thousand clergy in America. It included a letter from Rev. Moon when he was in Danbury prison and a paperback book titled God's Warning to the World. In many cities in my region, I met with ministers who had received the packet.

A second project was initiated in September of the following year when our movement launched a ten-million signature campaign to call attention to the threat of communism. In our region we gathered more than eight hundred thousand signatures. The purpose was to draw attention to the flaws of Marxist thought and the pitfalls of communist regimes.

I prayed with some ministers at the rock of tears in Korea.

Ministerial work in Philadelphia

Civic Outreach

Given his concern to save America from moral degradation and help people to develop a personal relationship with God, Reverend Moon was also keenly aware of the influence that policymakers had in the public square. In January of 1987, he chose fifty leaders to join a new advocacy organization under the supervision of Dr. Bo Hi Pak. That group brought thousands of public officials and civic leaders to educational seminars that focused on returning to the moral values advocated by America's founding fathers and on the dangers of communism.

In December of 1986, while I was present at the old mansion on the East Garden Estate, Dr. Pak told me that Reverend Moon had asked him to start an advocacy group. The purpose was to promote God, freedom, faith, and family in America. Dr. Pak asked my opinion on how best to implement that initiative. I suggested that he use the word "coalition" and establish two not-for-profit organizations: a 501 (c)(3) and a 501 (c)(4). Those two organizations would then be able to work with leaders from every socio-political perspective. They conducted educational seminars for public officials and policymakers on topics related to upholding democratic values and institutions. After consulting with others, Dr. Pak chose the names "American Constitution Committee" and "American Freedom Coalition."

Since I was a teenager, I was interested in public policy and current events. In the spring of 1968, while at Syracuse University, I campaigned in New Hampshire and New York for the presidential campaign of U.S. Senator Eugene McCarthy, who opposed America's war in Vietnam. Ironically, after joining the Unification Church later that same year, I became politically more conservative and anti-communist. Indeed, I worked for an organization that was affiliated with our church called the Freedom Leadership Foundation, which was an educational advocacy organization that opposed in a non-violent manner communist aggression throughout the world.

In the 1980s, I wanted to work for the American Freedom Coalition. However, Dr. Pak told me that when he had asked Reverend Moon if I could work with AFC, Father Moon said, "No! I want him to be a church leader." God seems to have had another plan for my life, which I accepted!

I was often present at the breakfast table when Reverend Moon announced fresh new initiatives. Thankfully, there was always a Korean who was present who translated Father Moon's comments for me. On two occasions, Father Moon indicated he wanted me to teach at Unification Theological Seminary. Yet, since UTS already had a full-time professor of church history, there was no full-time position for me there. As a result, I taught only one course per semester, while I was a vice president of the church.

Importance of Education

Rev. and Mrs. Moon were obsessed in a good way with the importance of members having an education that is grounded in the word of God. Leaders of our church received frequent training in the basic tenets of the Divine Principle, and there was always something new to learn.

An unusual educational program took place in August of 1987. Church leaders attended a 40-day workshop on the teachings of the Divine Principle in the grand ballroom of the New Yorker Hotel. The lecturer, Chang Seong Ahn, was an early disciple of Reverend Moon, who employed a Confucian, rote memory style of education. He viewed the mind of each student as being a blank slate, waiting to be filled with knowledge and understanding from the master teacher.

Reverend Ahn asked us to memorize his presentations word-for-word. That required a significant adjustment in my American way of thinking, since I had always been accustomed to thinking critically. It was difficult to adjust to a rote method of education. For me, that approach was unfamiliar and an eye-opener. It helped me to understand the Confucian mind and the traditional Chinese method of education. Most importantly, that seminar provided me with time to reflect, mature spiritually, and repent for my past sins and mistakes.

The Divine Principle Slide Show

Lecturers on the Divine Principle yearned for better teaching materials. I was given the task to meet that need by creating a manual and graphic aids. In 1986 the *Text for the Divine Principle Slide Show* was published by the church. I was happy to have developed it, but unfortunately it was not widely used.

Since producing a slide show was a new undertaking for our church, I worked with a software company to do the graphic design for the presentation. Regrettably for the designer, the tenets and terminology of Unification theology were strange and incomprehensible. Since he did not have a theological background, he had trouble depicting graphically the most basic doctrines of our church. As a result, I had to personally guide him as he made each drawing.

CHAPTER 29

Shifts in Lifestyle

At the Blessing of 2,075 couples at Madison Square Garden, many Americans were wed. That resulted in the need for adjustments in the polity and culture of our church. Many of the couples who had been in that Blessing at MSG lived in different places. It took some time for a movement of single adults who were living communally to transition into a family-centered church. Initially, the spouses returned to their previous missions in separate locations. That meant they had to develop their marital relationships long distance.

Church leaders felt that allowing many spouses simultaneously to move in order to start their married lives would disrupt the work of the church, even though these couples ultimately were destined to be the foundation of a new family-centered world order. Yet, because the regional directors did not want to lose members, those leaders discouraged them from moving. As a result, a deadlock existed in which couples were unable to get together to start their families. Special situations were given some consideration, but as time moved on, it seemed that it was necessary to do something to help the couples to begin their married lives.

I observed this conundrum with great concern and made an overall plan in which all of the wives would move simultaneously to where their husbands lived. I assembled a list of couples who were separated and their geographic locations, then prepared a comprehensive plan to unite many of the couples. I created a win-win solution in which each region would gain some members and lose others. I endeavored to balance evenly the gains and losses for each region and was sensitive to the plight of the couples, as well as to the concerns of the ten regional leaders.

I took the plan to Reverend Kwak, and he agreed to take the proposal to Reverend Moon for the founder's approval. In December of 1986, I went with Reverend Kwak to the East Garden Estate where he discussed the proposal with Rev. Moon. I sat in the small waiting room in the old mansion talking with Dr. Pak, while Rev. Kwak talked with Father Moon about our proposal. I anticipated that it would take a long time to obtain a decision. However, within a few minutes Rev. Kwak returned and said that Father Moon had approved the entire list of women who were to join their husbands. Apparently, it was the opportune time to propose a solution to the impasse. I was so happy to be instrumental in helping to bring more than four hundred couples together to begin their married lives.

Reverend Moon, like other prophets, received divine revelations. However, some people may assume that Reverend Moon never discussed his revelations and plans with his closest disciples before announcements were made. That is neither my experience nor understanding. Rev. Moon constantly received revelations from God, yet often he discussed significant issues with his closest disciples.

For me, rather than try to discuss an idea spontaneously on the spur of the moment with Reverend Moon, since I do not speak Korean, usually I presented my proposals in advance to one of his trusted disciples who introduced the topic to Reverend Moon. Then I would respond, if Father Moon asked my opinion. In that way, I was able to communicate the concerns of American members to our founder, but I kept all of those conversations confidential.

Neil Salonen, the president of our American church, recalled the following episode: In 1975 Reverend Moon sent many American missionaries around the world. In advance, he asked President Salonen to prepare a list that assigned each of them to a nation. Neil did so, and Father Moon approved the list. Later, when Neil made a few adjustments in the assignments, one missionary contended that Neil did not have the authority to make any revisions. Of course, he did not know that Neil had obtained carte blanche authority from Rev. Moon to act as he thought best in making assignments. Those who worked closely with Father Moon were often part of the decision-making process that preceded public announcements.

CHAPTER 30

Careers of our Children

In 1988 Nora and I sold our New Jersey property and bought a house in Irvington, NY where transportation by train to Manhattan was quick and convenient. The property was located in proximity to the East Garden Estate, where the Moon family lived, and also to the Belvedere Estate, where Sunday Services were held.

Our children went to public schools where some church friends were also students. Andrea and Chris left a mark at Irvington Senior High School, participating in various clubs and painting two large murals in the corridor. Andrea graduated in 1989. One year later, Chris graduated. In 1993 Ameri graduated from Governor Mifflin Senior High School in Shillington, Pennsylvania. High graduated from McLean Senior High School in Virginia in 1995. Those graduation ceremonies in different high schools indicate the moves that our family made in the 1990s.

It was time for our children to go to college. Happily, each of them chose a good career path. Andrea was a quiet achiever who won many awards in high school.

Interested in textile design, Andrea selected Fashion Institute of Technology in NY City and graduated in 1991. She and her husband, Tim Porter, moved to the Hudson River Valley after twenty years working in Manhattan and traveling to various nations, Andrea became a partner in a construction company that renovates houses.

Chris has a brilliant, creative mind. In May of 1992 he graduated summa cum laude from Cornell University. His initial interest was film-making, but after becoming disillusioned with the process of making movies, he decided to pursue a career as the senior software engineer for a company that manages and does bookings for high-end hotels worldwide. Chris and his wife, Mary, and their son, Ari (age 13), live in Seattle, Washington. As a hobby, Chris writes songs and produces music videos.

Ameri also graduated from the Fashion Institute of Technology in 1995 and became an interior designer. She also is artistic and creative. Ameri travels to NY City, the Hamptons, and other locations to lend her design skills to high-end clients. Ameri and her husband, Mike, live in the Hudson River Valley near Andrea and Tim.

High graduated from college with a degree in inventory and supply chain management after he and his family settled in Florida. He became the associate manager for a very large company that produces lasers for the U.S. government and various corporations. He and his wife, Kim, have two sons, Brayden, and Jaxon, who are 11 and 6 years old. Their family lives in central Florida near us.

Our children singing

Our three grandsons, Ari, Brayden, and Jaxon

Andrea and Tim

Chris and Mary

Ameri and Mike

High and Kim

Family Outings

For Nora and me, it was important to achieve synergy between our professional and personal lives by seeking to balance mission and family responsibilities. Our lives were not all work. There were some times to relax. Our family took occasional trips, spending time with relatives and church friends. When our children were growing up, we traveled to my aunt and uncle's ranch in Missouri and sometimes to Disney World in Orlando, Florida. We often visited our parents and siblings.

My parents held family reunions at my aunt and uncle's ranch. My children and their cousins have continued that tradition, gathering periodically in different locations. Many times we visited Nora's family in Lancaster County, Pennsylvania, which is the center of Amish and Mennonite country.

We went on some vacations with our children. Once we stayed in a rented house in Cape Cod, MA with three other families. That was a way to bond together and create long-lasting relationships. Another time the Jones, Edwards, and Spurgin couples stayed in adjacent timeshare units in a resort in the Pocono Mountains. It was a great experience for the adult children who visited us there. On the Fernwood golf course, I got my first hole-in-one, which surprised me. For a birthday gift, Andrea made a wall display of the ball, tee, and photo of the course.

In June of 2010, in celebration of our 40th wedding anniversary, Nora and I took an 8-day, round-trip cruise from Seattle to Alaska and back. The Jones and Edwards couples accompanied us on the cruise. It was a relaxing, enjoyable, and educational experience. We spent a delightful week sightseeing in Alaska and sharing stories with our best friends. After forty years, there was much to talk and laugh about, as we reminisced about our shared experiences. Of course, while in Seattle, we spent time with Chris, Mary, and Ari, and David and Takeko Hose.

Nora and I in Alaska

CHAPTER 31

Vice President

Reverend Moon convened a conference of two hundred leaders at the East Garden Estate on December 20, 1988, in which new national leaders for our church were elected. Dr. Mose Durst was chosen as the chairman of the Board of Directors, Dr. James Baughman as the president, and Dr. Tyler Hendricks and I as vice presidents. Each of us had a Ph.D. degree. I have been on the Board of Trustees of our national church ever sense that date.

In January of 1989 Dr. Baughman initiated a "Re-Awakening of the American Church" tour for church members in several cities. I was happy for the opportunity to speak at those internal revivals and to connect with my friends in the mission field.

James Baughman, myself, and Tyler Hendricks.

Speaking at a Re-Awakening rally

A speaking tour

One year later in February and March of 1990, I led an evangelical team and spoke primarily to college students on university campuses in eight states. Speaking on the topic, "God's Hope for America," I communicated an optimistic message regarding the future of America. Dr. Baughman and Dr. Hendricks toured other regions with their outreach teams. Over a span of six weeks, my 12-member team visited eight university campuses in Austin, Oklahoma City, Little Rock, Omaha, Sioux Falls, Fargo, Minneapolis, and Chicago respectively.

My speech in Chicago before students and some ministers.

The Children's Olympics

Private Excursions

Sometimes the Moon couple invited a few church leaders to accompany them on private excursions. I went with them to two movies in Manhattan and to Six Flags Great Adventure Theme Park in New Jersey. That allowed me to get to know them better. They were definitely outstanding role models. Indeed, they sought to experience every facet of life. Whatever they did was with faith, love, and fortitude.

Nora and I attended hundreds of church celebrations and events, and we ate many meals with our founders. In 1989 the church bought a property in Deer Park, Pennsylvania, which was named the New Hope Farm Equestrian Center. We attended an Autumn Classic Equestrian event there in September of 1991. Watching Rev. Moon ride a horse caught my attention; it was probably his first riding experience. It indicated his willingness to go outside of his comfort zone. Father Moon's exploration of every aspect of life gave opportunities for my wife and me to participate in a variety of interesting programs. Sometimes our children accompanied us, which gave them exciting experiences as well.

CHAPTER 32

Peacemaking

Moscow Summit

Reverend Moon was a staunch anti-communist; however, politically he was exclusively neither liberal nor conservative. His beliefs have an affinity with both perspectives. He met with leaders from both points of view in order to achieve peace and coined the term "head wing" to describe his divine, transcendent understanding. The liberal-conservative pair are two sides of the same coin. Both have ideological roots in the enlightenment views of 18th century Europe.

For Reverend Moon, Marxism-Leninism is a flawed theory. It is atheistic, materialistic, and socially divisive. Based on a false premise, communism espouses an incorrect understanding of reality. Yet, without compromising his beliefs, Reverend Moon was open to peaceful dialogue with communist leaders. With that frame of mind, he met in the 1990s with the supreme leaders of the Soviet Union and of North Korea. When Reverend Moon met with them and with other communist officials, he spoke about God and explained the flaws that are inherent in Marxist thought. Some church members developed an excellent, ideological critique and counterproposal to communism.

There are times when amazing opportunities present themselves.

To accompany Reverend and Mrs. Moon on a historic, 8-day visit to Moscow in April of 1990 was an exciting adventure. Reverend Moon's purpose was to pursue peaceful reconciliation between the communist and democratic worlds. In order to help promote peace between America and the Soviet Union, he met with Mikhail Gorbachev, the premier of the Union of Soviet Socialist Republics (USSR). He sought to find non-violent ways in which to reduce tensions between the two antagonists.

So it was that I found myself in Moscow, the capital of the USSR, as a part of a peacemaking visit. The first Summit Council for World Peace and the eleventh World Media Conference were held there with several hundred participants. The first lady, Raisa Gorbachev, attended a performance by the "Little Angels" children's choir. Each morning in a hotel suite, we prayed with the Moon couple, and Rev. Moon spoke to us. He declared that his visit was historic and would have a positive impact on world affairs.

The two conferences were followed by a private meeting for Reverend and Mrs. Moon with Premier Mikhail Gorbachev. I was not part of that very small group that met with Mr. Gorbachev in his Kremlin office. Yet my understanding is that meeting was significant in that it opened the USSR to religious freedom, which helped to liberate people from the oppression of a communist dictatorship.

Our conferences were featured on Soviet television stations. I was impressed with the friendly reception that Premier Gorbachev and his wife, Raisa, gave to our founders. Mikhail Gorbachev had initiated the Perestroika and Glasnost reforms. He was definitely the right man to be standing at the door when the iron curtain crumbled and the USSR opened its gates to the world.

Our staff left Moscow with the hope that soon in the future there would be an era of peace and prosperity. Sadly, reconciliation has taken longer than we anticipated it would take.

Reverend and Mrs. Moon with Premier Mikhail Gorbachev

North Korea

In December of 1991, Reverend Moon met with Kim Il Sung, the president of North Korea. With a smile on his face, Rev. Moon called President Kim his elder brother, even though he had been brutally tortured in North Korea. Thereafter, he arranged for our church-related businesses to make large investments in the development of the Democratic People's Republic of Korea (DPRK), which is the official name of North Korea.

A very small entourage accompanied the Moon couple to North Korea for a historic visit. It was a courageous move, given that they did not know what to expect. Soon after his arrival, Rev. Moon explained clearly and powerfully to several top North Korean officials that communism is based on an incorrect, atheistic ideology. Nevertheless, soon after that initial meeting, Reverend Sun Myung Moon met President Kim Il Sung. Reverend Moon had no intention to take revenge against Kim. Rather they embraced as brothers, and he called Kim his elder brother. That friendly gesture must have reached all the way to the throne of God!

Reverend Moon with President Kim Il Sung

Visit to Bulgaria

In September of 1990, after the fall of the Soviet empire, followers in America were asked by Reverend Moon to go to another nation for 40 days as a pioneer missionary. Presumably, the purpose was to support the globalization of our movement. In the process, we also were able to broaden our understanding of another nation.

I went to Bulgaria in October and November of 1990—wondering what I can do during a short visit. It is fortunate that God had a plan. The timing was amazing. Bulgaria was in the process of transitioning from communism to democracy. That trip turned out to be one of the most exciting times in my life. I went with a feeling that God was with me and there was no reason for me to be insecure or anxious.

In the early 1970s the first Unification missionary to Bulgaria, which was a communist nation, was Christian Zwerger from Austria. Christian has an amazing story in which God guided him to speak to a female college student who became the first Unification member in that nation, and she invited her friends to hear the lectures on the Divine Principle. Ironically, her father was the director of the internal security agency for the entire nation.

The mother of my friend, Henri Schauffler, connected me with a high-level contact in Sofia, the capital city. She was a very sophisticated, older woman who became my gracious host. She enriched my visit by presenting me to her influential friends. By God's grace, doors opened for me to meet prominent leaders of the emergent, anti-communist movement in Bulgaria.

For me that transformational period in Bulgaria's history was a very exciting time. One of her contacts was the thirty-nine-year-old, editor-in-chief of a Bulgarian television station who introduced me to many leaders in parliament and in the president's office. My Bulgarian friend seemed to know all of the top leaders in the nation. Everywhere we went, he testified to our movement, saying, "These are the finest people I've ever met, and we need to learn more about Reverend Moon and his movement for change." Such a wonderful person opened doors for me in every level of Bulgarian society. One person can do amazing things in terms of connecting us with influential people.

In that way, I was able to talk about Rev. Moon and our movement with leaders in the mayor's office, parliament, professors, university deans, labor leaders, television personalities, and three anti-communist political parties. I did a fifteen-minute interview about our church movement with a reporter from a Bulgarian television station in which I displayed photos in a book about Reverend Moon and our movement.

A television interview in Bulgaria

I gave lectures on the Unification view of modern history to students on several university and high school campuses. At that time, college students were on a nationwide strike, in order to bring down the prime minister who was a communist. Yet I was able to give presentations to students at several universities and schools. At one university I spoke several times. Since the students were on strike, no classes were open. The only program available at that time was my lecture. A professor made arrangements for my lectures.

When I went to that university with a professor, we did not know whether we would be able to enter any of the buildings on the campus, since there was a possibility that some students might block us from entering. But that did not happen. In fact, I was able to speak publicly to large groups in the main building. Initially when I arrived only six students were in the auditorium. Then suddenly more than two hundred people rushed into the room. They had been at another location waiting to hear my presentation.

Students and faculty decided they could attend, since my lectures on religious history were not official college courses. Even though students had boycotted every other class on the campus, they came to my presentation. Over 250 students came to that initial lecture; over 100 students came to two subsequent presentations.

After each lecture, twenty or more students followed me into a faculty lounge. Each time for several hours, they asked questions about Rev. Moon and his worldview. They were thrilled to learn about God's dispensation through the ages and were happy to hear clear explanations on how God has been working throughout history to save humanity. They had no opportunity previously to learn about God. I also spoke to many students at two large high schools.

The Bulgarian experience was a significant highlight of my life. It stands out as a special time when I experienced personally the living God working to bring good people across my path. In Bulgaria, everywhere I went I was able to speak freely about God, Reverend Moon, and Unification theology. And it provided an opportunity to observe up close the transition from autocratic to democratic institutions. It was a time when there were daily rallies in the streets in opposition to the rule of the communist prime minister. Four days before I left the demonstrators succeeded. The prime minister and his entire cabinet resigned. His replacement was an anti-communist.

Upon returning home, I arranged for my newfound friend from Bulgaria and his wife to meet our founders at a reception that was held at the East Garden Estate. When Reverend Moon began to speak, my friend stood up and sat down on the floor in front of Rev. Moon and listened attentively to his message. It was exciting for him to meet a religious leader who had a clear vision of what the world should do at this critical time in world history. Seven of the Bulgarian political and media leaders, including my friend and his wife, heard presentations at a leadership conference in Washington that was sponsored by the American Freedom Leadership Seminar. They were impressed with the quality of our Unification leaders and members.

The experience in Bulgaria gave me a taste of what it is like to be a missionary and of the kinds of miracles that our Heavenly Father is able to perform on the front lines of the dispensation when we are willing to step into an unknown, seemingly dangerous situation. I am indebted to Henri's mother for introducing me to her friend who made my trip enjoyable and meaningful.

Bulgarian leaders meet Reverend and Mrs. Moon

CHAPTER 33

Hometown

When Reverend Moon spoke to a gathering of two thousand church members at the Belvedere Estate on July 28, 1991, he said he wanted us to return to our hometowns. As he descended from the stage, in English he exhorted me to "send them out." He wanted our members to become "tribal messiahs", aka, good neighbors and model citizens in their hometowns.

Reverend Moon advised us to take care of our aging parents and strengthen our relationships with our families. His homeland of Korea is a family-centered culture. Attendance to parents and grandparents is very important, and that tradition seemed to him to be lacking in America. The years of persecution in America often resulted in rifts between members and their parents. Now was the time to heal any misunderstandings or hard feelings.

Soon thereafter, the top leader of the Unification Church in America suddenly downsized the staff at the national headquarters, and Nora and I lost our positions. Nora was the director of the family department; I was a vice president. For us, the sudden loss of our jobs without any severance pay was quite a shock. That leader said we should go to our hometown, implying that Reverend Moon had said that we personally should go home. Later we learned that our founder simply had given the same overall direction for members to go home. He had not mentioned either Nora or me by name. Later we learned that we had been let go by that leader, in order to downsize the size of the payroll at the church's national headquarters.

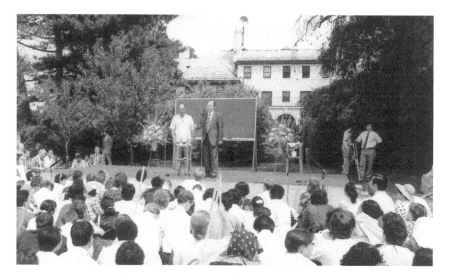

Reverend Moon's speech about hometown

Nevertheless, we faithfully went to our hometown, even though that was not very easy to do quickly. It was especially painful and difficult for our teenage children who suddenly were separated from their friends and school environment. Nora and I understood the financial need for our church to downsize, but we were hurt by the insensitive way in which we were treated. For us, the Supreme Being is a God of love. That faith in a loving Heavenly Parent carried us through a very uncertain and troublesome period in our lives.

Nora and my lives have been filled for decades with many ups and downs, but this was the most challenging situation that we had ever faced. It was a deeply disturbing and painful time. Indeed, it was the low point in our lives. I felt like I was facing the same types of trials and tribulations that Job had experienced.

I was forty-six. After having worked for the church for more than two decades, suddenly Nora and I had to find another way to support our family. Without jobs or savings, we faced financial distress. As a result, we declared bankruptcy and did a short sale of our house, aka, sold it at a low price. Although we had hit rock bottom, we were determined not to give up.

During such a time of unbelievable personal turmoil, our faith in God and our intuition guided us. I worked on several part-time jobs while looking for a good place to settle our family. But it was hard to find a full-time, professional position. It was a time when many universities and organizations were downsizing. There were very few employment openings either in academia or with nonprofits. Many qualified candidates, who were middle-aged men like myself, were applying for every available job.

The funny card I sent to Nora

Temporarily, Nora moved with our children into two rooms on a property owned by the church and taught English to Japanese women. Andrea was in college; Chris was a senior in high school. Ameri and High were enrolled in local public schools.

I went to Terre Haute, Indiana to live with my parents, but there were no job openings there. I sent a funny card to Nora about Terre Haute being "nowheresville," which helped to lift our spirits. During the Christmas season, I went to St. Louis and sold marquetry inlay pictures in a shopping mall. I stayed with a couple who were church members and sold a piece of art to Uncle Pete and Aunt Gloria.

After that experience, I returned to the east coast. With Father Moon's approval, Nora and I moved our family to Pennsylvania, near her home, where I did temporary jobs while searching for full-time employment.

A Wake-Up Call

Living a life of dedication to a higher purpose has been meaningful and fulfilling for Nora and me. It has consisted of wholesome friendships and activities for our children. We trusted that our children would be okay when they attended church programs. Sadly, in January of 1992 a group of Unification-born second-generation teenagers were involved in a tragic vehicle accident. After attending a church workshop, they had decided to go to a movie in Westchester County, NY. The 15-seat van, carrying twenty-two youth, overturned after a thunderstorm on the Saw Mill River Parkway. David Ang and our 17-year-old daughter, Andrea, were thrown out of the rear door.

Nora and I were in Pennsylvania visiting her parents and exploring places to move our family. We returned when Chris notified us of the vehicle accident. It was a long trip. Keeping in touch meant occasionally stopping at a phone booth to find out what was happening.

When we arrived at the hospital, we were told David had passed away. We were saddened when we heard that the 18-year-old David had died. It was a tragic loss. Andrea was hospitalized with minor injuries. Ameri was okay, but she was shocked when she saw Andrea seemingly unconscious. Chris chose not to go since the van was overcrowded. For us, that accident was disconcerting. It was a wake-up call for us not to take life for granted. It demonstrated the necessity to supervise our children more closely.

CHAPTER 34

Women for World Peace

In March of 1992, Mother Moon spoke at the inaugural rally for the Women's Federation for World Peace at the Olympic Stadium in Seoul. One hundred sixty thousand women attended. Previously, Father Moon announced to our members that we are living in the age of women and declared that Mother Moon would become the international leader of the Women's Federation for World Peace. In May of 1992, Nora became the first president of WFWP in the United States.

Nora grew up in the Mennonite Church, which is a historic peace denomination. Working with women in a cause that is devoted to peace fits her disposition and religious background. I was proud of Nora. I never hesitated to support my wife in her many providential missions.

As president of the Women's Federation, Nora developed close friendships with many celebrities and public officials. She was instrumental in organizing in America "Sisterhood Ceremonies" that included Bridge of Peace Crossings, which was her idea. Those heartwarming crossings created a forum for friendship and peace between women from different backgrounds. Ladies reached out in friendship to women from another race, religion, and/or nationality. Tens of thousands of women around the globe participated in those ceremonies that sought to build bridges, not conflict between people.

During Bridge of Peace Crossings in eight Sisterhood Ceremonies, 4,000 Japanese women partnered with 4,000 American "sisters" to heal the pains from the past. As the most significant aspect of those ceremonies, many American women, including former first lady Barbara Bush, crossed the bridge to meet a "sister" from Japan. As Mrs. Bush descended the stairs that led to the stage, she clasped the hand of her newfound friend. As former President George H.W. Bush watched his wife on the stage, he said to Nora with tears in his eyes, "If we would have done this 50 years ago, we may have prevented a war." Thereafter, President Bush spoke movingly to the audience about the need to bring about peace.

Nora with former President George H.W. and First Lady Barbara Bush and Mrs. Motoko Sugiyama

CHAPTER 35

Moving

Pennsylvania

In February of 1992, Nora and I moved to Exton, Pennsylvania with our two younger children. For us, that was the most difficult time in our lives. Our older children, Andrea and Chris, were students at the Fashion Institute of Technology and Cornell University, respectively. As a middle school student, the transition for our daughter Ameri wasn't easy. She knew no one at her new school and missed her friends in New York. Soon thereafter High went to Seoul to study the Korean language.

The following year we moved to Shillington, Pennsylvania. Keiko and Keimei Sugiyama lived with us. Their mother, Motoko, who worked closely with Nora, was President of WFWP in Japan. Because Motoko was working on the sisterhood ceremonies in America, she wanted to be near her teenage daughters. Ameri, High, Keiko, and Keimei went to high school there. Ameri graduated from Shillington High School and became a student at Fashion Institute of Technology.

It was while we were there that Nora became the president of the Women's Federation for World Peace, USA. She worked in New York City at the WFWP headquarters on Mondays and Tuesdays. On Wednesdays, she was at home in Pennsylvania for one day where she worked in a nursing home as a psychological consultant. On Thursdays through Sundays, she was in Washington organizing Bridge of Peace ceremonies sponsored by WFWP.

Nora traveled back-and-forth by bus, since we needed our car at home. For her, it was a grueling schedule, but working with women leaders was satisfying. It was a very difficult time for us financially. I did telemarketing and sold sports paraphernalia at retail stores until I found a job in Washington, DC in 1994 when I was 49 years of age.

Balancing Mission and Family Life

The challenge was how to balance our lives as responsible parents while continuing to work long hours and travel on church-related missions. We did the best we could to care for our precious children while remaining steadfast in our faith commitment. Though we had very little money, we tried not to let our children know that we were struggling financially, but it became obvious in the early 1990s. When we declared bankruptcy and moved out of our home, it was impossible to shield them from the reality of our financial difficulties.

Bright Light: The Marriage of our Children

The Reverend and Mrs. Moon officiated at the Blessing of 30,000 couples in the Seoul Olympic Stadium on August 23, 1992. Nora was asked to take care of the American couples who participated in the ceremony, including many biracial couples. It was a happy time for our family. Our daughter, Andrea, and Tim Porter participated. As teenagers, they had attended the Little Angels Art School at the same time. They were happy to learn that Rev. Moon had matched them. Nora and Andrea made the wedding dress. In fact, Andrea finished the sewing by hand on the plane. Rev. Martin and Mrs. Marion Porter, and Nora and I, watched our daughter and son-in-law begin their married life, and we were very happy.

Three years later, 360,000 couples participated in a Blessing that was held in the same stadium on August 25, 1995. Participating in that event were couples who were not members of the Unification Church. To our delight our son, Chris, and Ko-Francoise Blanchard from France were wed. We were proud of them as they began their married life. Later, however, Chris and Ko were divorced, and Chris was blessed in marriage to Mary Hose. They have one son, Ari, and live in Seattle near Mary's parents, Reverend David and Mrs. Takeko Hose, who were also married in 1970 in the 777 Blessing ceremony.

Our children, their spouses, and oiur three grandsons.

A Virginia Home

From 1994 through 1996, I worked as the production manager for *The Washington Golf Monthly*, a magazine owned by *The Washington Times*. On weekdays, I lived in Maryland with Dan and Susan Fefferman.

On weekends, I went home. Keiko and Keimei Sugiyama lived there with Ameri, High, Nora, and I. Keimei said that ours was a happy household, even though my wife and I were busy and often traveling. At school, the four teenagers participated in an environmental club and in other activities. They especially enjoyed performing in major roles in school plays.

We enjoyed sharing our home with the Sugiyama girls. The presence of Keiko and Keimei was very comfortable for us as it was for their mother, Motoko, who was president of WFWP in Japan. Nora worked closely with Motoko in organizing many Bridge of Peace ceremonies held between Japanese and American women.

In July of 1995, we moved our family to McLean, Virginia, since Nora and I were both working in Washington DC. We rented two rental trucks: one to carry my books; the other for everything else. Our children helped us to make the move, including our son-in-law who drove one of the trucks. Later, one of our children said, "I am never going to move your books again." For me, those books were precious possessions, but eventually I gave several thousand of them away.

High and Keimei lived with us in northern Virginia near Washington DC. They graduated from McLean Senior High School. Chris lived there briefly before attending Cornell University. High's part-time job in a bookstore was a nice outlet for him; he likes to serve people. He enjoyed observing parents buying books for their children.

Adopting a Mission Country

For forty days in August and September of 1996, Nora and Betsy Jones attended the first national messiah workshop at the Cheongpyeong Training Center in South Korea. Although Farley and I had full-time jobs, we participated in the final ten days of that program.

On the final day of the workshop, each couple was assigned a nation to adopt, visit, and serve to the best of their ability. Father Moon called the couples who completed the workshop "national messiahs," elevating their status from "tribal messiahs" to the national level. Nora and I were assigned to Nicaragua. In November of 1996, we visited and prayed for Nicaragua in order to determine how we could support the church there.

Nora with church members in Nicaragua

CHAPTER 36

A School is Born

The University of Bridgeport in Connecticut had serious financial troubles. In May of 1992, Professors World Peace Academy signed an agreement with UB to provide the university with substantial funding in exchange for PWPA having the right to appoint a majority of the members of the UB Board of Trustees. That money saved the University of Bridgeport from bankruptcy. Under that arrangement, for the next twenty-five years, the university flourished.

Having observed the educational needs of youth in Nicaragua, Nora and I met with two administrators at the University of Bridgeport regarding the possibility of arranging an online, distance learning program for students in Nicaragua. During that conversation, they asked many questions about our teenage children and the arrangements we had made for their formal education.

In December of 1996, Reverend Moon asked me to start a senior high school on the campus of the University of Bridgeport. Apparently, those two university officials had recommended me for that role. Establishing a new residential, secondary school became a consuming, yet fulfilling, responsibility that defined the next two decades of my life. In January of 1997, I became the headmaster of New Eden Academy, which later became known as the college preparatory school "where students meet the world."

For six months, while my family was in Virginia, I worked in Connecticut to set up a private high school. In June of 1997, after High and Kemei graduated from McLean High School, Nora and I moved our family to an apartment in Bridgeport. As president of the Women's Federation for World Peace, Nora commuted from there to her office in New York City. High lived with us. He became a manager of a local movie theater and took a few college courses.

Nora and I

Education is Decentralized in America

Unlike other nations, education in America is decentralized. The U.S. Constitution does not mention education as being within the purview of the federal government. The 10th Amendment to the Constitution has been interpreted by the U.S. Supreme Court to mean that education is primarily a state responsibility. The U.S. government's involvement in education started in 1867; in 1979 the U.S. Department of Education was established. Yet, elementary and secondary education have always been the responsibility of the states. Each state and municipality has its own educational standards and health and safety regulations for schools.

Establishing a private high school in Bridgeport, which is certified by the state government was difficult to do, since Connecticut has many hundreds of pages of health and safety regulations that govern boarding schools in which the students are minors.

Establishing a Residential School

Educating teenagers was a rewarding, yet trying experience. Even though I loved that mission, it was difficult to have our boarding school certified by the state government. According to our attorney, our academy was the first new private, residential high school founded in Connecticut in more than four decades. By the grace of God and support of our founders, we were able to create an excellent school, in spite of the many hundreds of pages of bureaucratic regulations.

Every step that we took was a challenge and a learning experience. Although this was a new role for me, I knew that I had the necessary legal skills and knowledge of how government agencies operate that was needed to obtain the necessary approvals, and I had the administrative and financial skills to run the school.

An Agreement with the University of Bridgeport

New Eden Academy rented two facilities from the University of Bridgeport: Cooper Hall which is a dormitory that we converted into a residential high school, and Wisteria, a Victorian-style house.

The international church provided an initial grant of $1 million to establish the school. Those funds were used to convert Cooper Hall into classrooms, offices, and dormitories. The first floor consisted of offices, a health center, classrooms, and an apartment for a teacher's family. The second floor consisted of a girls' dorm; the third of a boys' dorm; the fourth provided housing for faculty, staff, and university graduate students who rented rooms from the school. Nora and I lived in an apartment in a separate building that was owned by the school.

As the leader of New Eden Academy, I signed an agreement to use facilities on the university campus in exchange for a monthly fee based on the number of students who were enrolled each school year. That arrangement included access to many university facilities: the dining hall, recreation center, library, theaters, music room, classrooms, science laboratories, ceramics studio, the gymnasium, and an auditorium in the student center. It was a pact that has lasted for more than twenty-five years and continues to exist. In addition, our students were able to take university courses. That allowed the students to obtain college credits while still in high school. Later we amended the contract to include use of a new soccer field.

Although we were a small school, that alliance with the university gave the students access to many venues at U.B. for a wide range of programs and activities, including sports and school plays. The university administrators and I were pleased with that mutually beneficial accord. Many of the students, who were Unification-born second-generation youth, were very intelligent, creative, and talented. Having a place and opportunity for them to express themselves was valuable.

A mathematics professor, who previously had taught at the United States Military Academy, wrote a letter to the president of the university, complaining about two of our students who were enrolled in an advanced calculus course. When those two brothers, who were from South Korea, had the highest scores on a mid-term examination, that professor assumed that they had cheated. He asked them to stand at the blackboard in front of the class to solve several very complex problems, which they did correctly. That tenured professor became an ardent proponent of our school.

CHAPTER 37

Government Certification

Church Donation

The church gave New Eden Academy an initial grant of $1 million as a startup plus monthly support. However, in January of the second school year, additional monthly grants were discontinued, which made it difficult financially to survive as a school.

Connecticut does not have a voucher system, which provides money from the state government to pay for a student to attend either a private or a parochial school. Our academy had no endowment and was not tuition-driven. Recruiting paying students was difficult, since the parents who were rank-and-file church members did not have the money to send their children to a private, residential school. It is fortunate that we were able to keep tuition and fees very low, by renting apartments to university graduate students at the Seaside Institute building and renting rooms in Cooper Hall. With that rental income, the school was able to survive.

Health Regulations for a Boarding School

A residential school needs classrooms, offices, dormitories, faculty, students, policies, handbooks, books, supplies, and technology. In addition, in order to be certified, it is imperative that a school obtain numerous permits from many state and municipal government agencies. One year before I became the headmaster, a church member researched the procedures that are required to obtain state approval for a private school. By mistake, she did not tell the officials at the Connecticut Department of Education that our intention was for New Eden Academy to be a boarding school. Since the students were minors, the school was required to abide by many hundreds of pages of health and safety regulations

In May of 1997, in the process of making plans to open the academy in September, I was shocked to learn that it was necessary for a residential high school to obtain from the Connecticut Board of Education an exemption from many of those onerous state health and safety mandates, in order to obtain approval for minors to live in a school dormitory.

Unfortunately, the deadline had already passed to apply to obtain an exemption by September. Moreover, it was not possible for our application requesting an exemption to be placed on the agenda of the state Board of Education until December of 1997. That predicament put us in a quandary. I decided to proceed with plans to open the school in September, and we made creative arrangements for students to live temporarily as homestays with local church families—until we could obtain approval to use our dormitories.

Our application for an exemption was scheduled to be considered by the Board of Education at its meeting in December. Aware of the controversies that surrounded Reverend Moon and our church, I was concerned that one or more members of the Board might oppose our application for exemption. Therefore, I hired an attorney, who was an expert in education law, to help our school if any concerns or objections were raised by the Board.

Thankfully, it was the holiday season, and there was a gleeful and friendly atmosphere. Suddenly, at the beginning of the meeting, our attorney said, "We can go." She explained that the superintendent of the Department of Education, whom we had met, had placed our request on the consent agenda. At the beginning of the session, all items that had been placed on that special agenda were unanimously approved without any objections, including our request for an exemption. Finally, we were allowed to use our newly furnished dormitories! I went home with a light heart! Robert Schwartz and Dr. Frederick Swarts were invaluable in helping Nora and I to establish the school.

More Health Mandates

However, for a boarding school additional health and safety regulations were still required, since the students are minors. For instance, the fact that we had established an infirmary meant that we were required to abide by many other administrative regulations.

Our school nurse was in contact with the Connecticut Department of Health daily regarding compliance with health regulations of the state government for residential schools. One day, she suddenly reported to me that the state officials were insisting that we must have a heliport available in case it was necessary to transport a student or teacher quickly to a hospital. I was shocked! I wondered, "Why would the government require that a small school have a heliport?" That seemed to me to be an unreasonable mandate.

We were relieved when our lawyer, who was a licensed nurse, informed us that the problem can be resolved by calling our facility "a health center." We did that, and the problem was solved, including the need for a heliport. I breathed a big sigh of relief when our attorney sent a formal letter to the Department of Health verifying that we had set up a health center with a locked cabinet to store medications and prescriptions. In this way, we were able to abide by Connecticut health and safety guidelines. With a grateful heart, I moved on to take care of our initial group of bright and talented students.

Opposition to Our School

A newspaper reporter suddenly appeared unannounced at our school. I was informed that he had already interviewed several students who were taking a high school class held in a university classroom. The article that he authored in *The New York Times* raised questions about the appropriateness and legality of a church school operating on a nonsectarian college campus. Soon thereafter, several television crews arrived at our school to investigate the relationship between our academy and the university.

Moreover, after reading the article in the *New York Times*, several directors of the Board of Trustees of the University of Bridgeport objected to our academy operating on the university's nonsectarian campus. The Executive Committee of the Board decided that in order to remain on the campus our school must either become nonsectarian or leave. That stipulation put a temporary strain on our relationship with the university, but we were able to solve the problem.

In response to the concerns of the university, in March of 2004 the Board of Trustees of New Eden Academy changed the name of the school to Bridgeport International Academy and adopted a new charter and bylaws. With Reverend Moon's consent, the school was transformed into a nonsectarian academy open to students of all religions, races, nationalities, and ethnicities. Furthermore, the school's motto became, "BIA is the place where students meet the world."

Reverend Moon spoke to me about the importance of creating in Bridgeport a model educational system from kindergarten through graduate school. In 1996 a group of mothers started Bridgeport Hope School, which was housed on the first floor of the Seaside Institute building. That grassroots endeavor became an excellent school that was able to be certified by the state government. That complemented the high school and university that existed in Bridgeport.

Regional Accreditation

In America, there is no national accrediting agency. Therefore, in 2003 New Eden Academy applied for accreditation on the highest level possible with a prestigious regional accrediting body, the New England Association of Schools and Colleges. For NEASC, we prepared an extensive self-study and hosted a visiting committee consisting of seven professional educators. Three years later in 2006, Bridgeport International Academy was granted full accreditation, which made the Reverend and Mrs. Moon and all of our stakeholders very happy. Obtaining approval from an accrediting body on that high a level was a major accomplishment—an aspiration achieved.

Our college preparatory school had domestic and international students from a wide diversity of religious, racial, ethnic, and cultural backgrounds. The objectives of BIA were to prepare students to be adults of high moral character, good citizens, and college graduates who engaged in meaningful careers. Our academy taught basic courses in English, mathematics, the natural sciences, and the social sciences. In addition, the school became known for academic excellence, character education, theatrical performances, and the production of outstanding videos. The wonderful costumes for the plays were made by the faculty and staff.

Faculty and students

With students

Government Certification

Commencement

With players in a performance of A Midsummer Night's Dream

CHAPTER 38

Teenagers!

Discipline Problems

When I was asked to become headmaster, Nora commented to me that dealing with teenagers could be troublesome. I was more idealistic than my wife was, but very soon I realized that she was right. Being a church school brought students who were bright and talented, yet some of them had emotional baggage or had developed bad habits. Caring for teenagers, some of whom were testing the limits, was a challenging task that required wisdom, love, and patience. Nevertheless, being an educational leader was a meaningful, rewarding experience.

To institutionalize a desire for learning and a commitment to honesty and integrity among the students took several years to accomplish. We began the process by establishing high academic and moral standards of conduct. In the first three years, some students were expelled due to violations of the student code of conduct. It was gut-wrenching to do that, but it was necessary in order to maintain a high standard of behavior and avoid future problems. In protest, one student stood in front of our school's mini-van when I was trying to take her friend who was being expelled to the airport. It took patience, but finally I was able to send the girl home to her parents.

We believe that God helped and guided us in running the school. Nora surrounded the school with angelic energy. She asked the angels to protect each student, teacher, parent, and member of the staff. Ultimately, we were able to be a positive influence in the lives of those teenagers. When I reflect on what happened, I am grateful for the support of my wife, the faculty, and the stakeholders in building a school where youth could learn and become mature in a wholesome atmosphere.

Municipal Property Taxes

The Seaside Institute, which housed BIA, was immediately adjacent to the University of Bridgeport. Church leaders purchased that facility and made three attempts to donate it to the University of Bridgeport. However, since the university had an overabundance of empty buildings, the administrators at UB refused those offers. So, the church donated that facility to our academy.

Originally the Seaside Institute was a school for teenage girls who worked in a local factory. In 1896 Frances Cleveland, the wife of the President of the United States, dedicated the building. In the 1940s, an addition was added for printing presses for a newspaper. In the 1980s, a developer converted the building into thirty condominiums, but he sold only one unit and went bankrupt. The U.S. Housing and Urban Development Agency took possession of the building. Our church bought it at an auction. Later our school purchased the one unit that previously had been sold.

Yet $245,000 was owed to the City of Bridgeport in back taxes, which was charging an annual interest rate of 19% on those unpaid taxes. In order to settle that debt with the city, I asked twenty-four banks to give us a mortgage, but they refused. Apparently, they were unwilling to loan money to our academy because they did not want to foreclose on a school. Finally, after perseverance, I secured a mortgage from a bank located in Long Island, NY. With that loan we were able to pay off the money owed in back taxes and the interest that had accumulated.

Yet, even though our school was a 501 (c)(3) nonprofit, tax-exempt corporation, for many months the tax accessor of the City of Bridgeport refused to give our school a property tax exemption. By the grace of God, that tax accessor (who had caused us so much trouble) eventually resigned, and our attorney arranged an out-of-court settlement in which the city recognized the tax-exempt, non-profit status of our school and agreed that BIA would no longer be required to pay property taxes on the Seaside Institute building.

CHAPTER 39

Changing Roles

Nora finished a seven-year term as the president of the Women's Federation for World Peace in 1999. Rev. Moon asked Nora to work with me at New Eden Academy, indicating he wanted a couple to be the leaders of the school. To seal that assignment, he asked us to kiss publicly in front of one hundred people who were gathered at the East Garden Estate. Although we were shy, we did it, and we were very happy to work together.

I was the Principal; Nora was Vice-Principal. She guided the faculty, students, and parents. I focused on administrative, financial, and legal issues. That division of labor was a very successful arrangement.

Step-by-step, we established an accredited school that consisted of a core curriculum and became known for academic excellence, character education, and community service. In addition, the school had signature programs in theater, video production, international studies, and the fine arts. Students had the option to study Spanish, Japanese, or Korean. After twenty years when we left the school, there was an outstanding faculty and staff consisting of many Unification-born second-generation leaders. Some of them were graduates of our academy who obtained a college degree and returned to teach at the academy. Along the way, we had many hundreds of very moving emotional experiences with students from a diversity of racial, national, and religious backgrounds.

Nora and me with Reverend Moon when she became the vice principal

Limited finances required that the salaries and benefits for faculty, staff, and ourselves be rather modest. Yet, the institution survived in spite of the financial limitations. Sometimes my wife and I kept the school alive and avoided financial exigency by donating our own personal funds to cover payroll and other expenses.

A Visit from the Founders

In June of 2003, when Reverend and Mrs. Moon visited the University of Bridgeport, I met them in the university library and invited them to visit BIA. They came to the school, and Father Moon wrote a school motto in Chinese calligraphy. An English translation of the motto is, "The determination of youth becomes the flower of an adult life."

Reverend Moon taps me on the head and says "good job".

Reverend Moon writing the motto for BIA in Chinese calligraphy

To understand Reverend Moon, it helps to be steeped in the Chinese classics, which was the language that was used by the literati of yore, which means in times long past, in Korea and in China. Sun Myung Moon was innovative and creative. He invented many new phrases, words, and names for people and places, often using either classical Chinese or Korean script.

On another occasion, I was the only American who was present when Rev. Moon went to the top of the university library. As he observed the city, he prayed and then claimed all of the land north of the Long Island Sound and south of Highway 95 to be used for God's purposes.

A summer in Brazil

In June of 1999, there was a 40-day church workshop in Brazil. Nora and I traveled to the New Hope Farm in Jardim, Brazil. Nora was the leader of eighty participants from America and Europe. Reverend Moon was interested in exploring the vast Pantanal region with its grasslands, tropical wetlands, and a sanctuary for plants, birds, and animals. He wanted people to experience the natural beauty of the region that surrounds the Paraguay River. When Reverend and Mrs. Moon visited the New Hope Farm, we took an official photo with them.

Nora becomes the Principal

Nora and I had a profound experience with Reverend Moon at the East Garden Estate on March 27, 2005. On that Easter Sunday, we were present at the breakfast table with the Jones and Ang couples. Reverend Moon began reminiscing about what he remembered about each of us during the early days of our church in America.

Suddenly, he asked Nora to become the principal of Bridgeport International Academy and for Betsy and Marie to assist her. Next, he spoke to Nora about his vision for the academy. I was happy that Rev. Moon had intervened and promoted Nora. I felt that what was important was for me not to be concerned and self-centered.

I sensed Nora becoming the principal meant that our school would have a new beginning. Father Moon then asked Dr. Chung Shik Yang to become the chairman of the Board of Directors of the Academy, which indicated his trust in our school.

Two days later at a gathering at the East Garden Estate, Reverend Moon asked the "Women of Bridgeport" (Nora, Betsy, and Marie) to stand up. Then he announced that he would ask the leaders of our international church to donate $2 million to BIA to construct a school facility. Everyone was amazed!

BIA received a donation for a new school building

Shortly afterward, Nora said her first decision was to ask me to remain as the president and continue to be responsible for administrative, legal, and financial affairs. Nora said her focus would be on the students, faculty, and parents, as well as on overall issues. That division of labor worked well. It used the skills of both of us for the benefit of the school. We served as parental figures for our academy.

My wife and I complemented each other; we worked well together. Even though our mission was complex and challenging, seeing students mature and prepare to go into the world was rewarding. Our high school graduated many outstanding students, who went to excellent universities and later were hired for good professional jobs. A few of them worked for the church. Every year as we said goodbye to another graduating class, with pride in our hearts we enjoyed seeing the students leave the nest, go to college, and prepare for meaningful lives and careers.

After investigating many properties that were available for purchase, Nora and I decided to renovate the Seaside Institute, which was the apartment building that the school owned. That stately old building originally had been established as a school for young girls. It was appropriate for it to be used again as an academy. Eighteen months after we received the donation from the international church, in September of 2006 our academy moved into a beautiful, newly renovated facility.

Two Hits from Mother Nature

Though it was unusual for a hurricane to hit Connecticut, in August of 2011 Hurricane Irene visited Bridgeport with a vengeance and flooded the first floor of the Seaside Institute building that housed Bridgeport Hope School, and seven apartments. Since BIA was located on the upper floors, the school itself was not flooded.

The next year in October, Hurricane Sandy made an unprecedented, even more devastating visit, causing $1.1 million in damages to the entire first floor of our school building. Thankfully, the academy had just acquired flood insurance two months before the storm hit, which provided the school with the necessary funds to repair the extensive damage and build a large multi-purpose room, which after Nora and I retired was named "Spurgin Hall."

*The Spurgin Hall Plaque in the Seaside Institute Building
at Bridgeport International Academy*

It is interesting that in 1998 I said to Father Moon that I want to construct a statue of him at the academy. He responded, "There will be many statues of me. Someday a statue of you will be built at your school." At that time, I laughed. Yet, now there is a plaque at the entrance to Spurgin Hall with an image of Nora and me as the founders of the school!

Reverend Moon asked me to create a residential high school. In the twenty years we spent there, we built an exemplary college preparatory academy. We saw teenagers from many nations learn and grow up. Almost all of them became responsible, mature adults, graduated from excellent universities, and found excellent careers. We had a talented, dedicated faculty and staff who won the hearts of the students, nurtured them, mentored them, and made a significant impact on their lives. We were pleased that many Unification-born second-generation teachers and staff are now working at the academy.

Nora and I continued to serve as leaders of BIA until January of 2019 when I became president of Unification Theological Seminary. Nora worked at the school for one more year. We needed a capable successor. Dr. Frank LaGrotteria commanded our attention. We had observed his support for the school as a parent and as a trustee, and we appreciated his administrative and technological skills. Based on our recommendation, the Board appointed Dr. LaGrotteria to be the new headmaster, and he was very successful. For several more years, Nora and I served as trustees of the Board of Directors of BIA. Frank's successor, Emily Kise, who is an accomplished young educator and administrator, originally was recruited by us as a teacher. Emily and her husband, Matt, who are a Unification-born second-generation couple, have done an excellent job, in spite of financial challenges and the difficulties due to the Covid-19 pandemic.

CHAPTER 40

Remembering Reverend Moon

On September 2, 2012 at ninety-two years of age, Reverend Sun Myung Moon passed away. A prophet for the ages who was chosen by God as a person of destiny, Reverend Moon was the consummate educator. He taught us how to live a good life and about the coming of a new age. His insightful teachings brought to light the hidden meaning of many passages in the Bible and provided detailed descriptions of the lives of biblical characters.

Reverend Moon's departure left a huge vacuum in my life. Having interacted closely with him for five decades, I can testify firsthand to his compassion, honesty, and integrity. I was there! Reverend Moon practiced what he preached. He strengthened my resolve and sense of responsibility to do what is right and to seek to bring about peace throughout the world. It is worth reaching for the heavens.

Though the altruistic goal of establishing an ideal world may seem like an impossible dream, Reverend Moon believed that God's plan to establish the kingdom of heaven on earth ultimately will be achieved. Eventually, society will be completely transformed, he said, into a world of harmony and peace—a "new heaven and a new earth." (Rev 21: 1) Such a transition would not come quickly or easily, but it is a promise from God that is destined to happen.

Evil is part of the human story. In the short run, evil is strong, yet the love of a benevolent God is more powerful. For Reverend Moon, the false precedes the true, but God has the last word. Our Heavenly Father, who is just and loving, allows the forces of evil to act first. What is spiritually and morally right will become apparent, and God will act to save all of humankind from its fallen state. Truth will prevail. The enemies of Jesus probably assumed that they had won a victory by having him crucified. Yet God resurrected Jesus, resulting in spiritual salvation for his believers.

Reverend Moon praying

Life is good. In spite of the wars, chaos and uncertainty of the contemporary world, I am optimistic about the future. I am confident that we will survive as a human race. God is love, and love will overcome hatred. The world is changing rapidly. Someday a peaceful world will become a reality, pushed forward by the lives and legacies of Father and Mother Moon.

I have learned much from the Moon couple and had many amazing and precious personal experiences with them. They are my mentors.

Reverend Moon endured false accusations, character assassination, torture, and unjust imprisonment in four nations. He never wanted to take revenge, but instead sought to leave a legacy of forgiveness and love. Nora and I grieved the loss of our spiritual leader who had a major impact on our lives and on millions of people worldwide.

The Successor

A woman of deep faith, Dr. Hak Ja Han Moon succeeded her late husband as the leader of the Unification Church worldwide. A farsighted leader, she has expanded on the legacy handed down from her husband. The leadership of Mother Moon represents a new stage in the progression of God's providence. She was seventeen when they married; he was forty. Mother Moon was loyal to her husband throughout their fifty-two years together. During that time, they were inseparable, working in tandem side-by-side in the quest for a peaceful world. Mother Moon was a co-founder of all of the Unification-affiliated organizations, even though her husband initiated most of them.

As a leader, Mother Moon has brought a feminine perspective to the movement. Having emphasized the need to establish a culture of peace, she declared that "Today's problems cannot be solved by the logic of power. . . . Our present problems can only be solved by the logic of love."

Dr. Hak Ja Han Moon

Mother Moon and her husband taught that God is masculine and feminine. After becoming the leader, she proclaimed that the motherly aspect of the Creator needs to be recognized and that God should be referred to as our "Heavenly Parent." In Genesis 1:27, it is written, "So God created man in his own image, in the image of God he created him; male and female he created them." Thus, the creation of man and woman was a physical manifestation of the polarity that exists within God.

Reverend Moon often stated that we are living in an age when women will play more prominent roles. He strove to elevate the role of women in the public square, which was very unusual for an Asian leader.

A Culture of Peace and Prosperity

The three primary goals of our founders have been to pursue interdependence, mutual prosperity, and universal moral values. Through the Universal Peace Federation, Mother Moon established numerous transnational forums for heads of state, religious leaders, and academics to promote universal values as a step toward lasting peace. Affectionately known by church members as the Mother of Peace, she has blessed millions of couples in holy marriages and has embraced many religious and political leaders, inviting them to speak at huge "Rallies of Hope."

Although Mother Moon's overall vision has been the same as that of her late husband, she brings her own unique personality, leadership style, concerns, and emphasis for the movement. Each leader makes changes indicating different interests and up-to-date understandings of God's providence at a particular time in history. After her husband passed away, Mother Moon consolidated the sacred texts and the holy days, and initiated several new traditions. Moreover, she elevated younger people to positions of leadership.

The Unification movement has never made constructing church buildings the highest priority—often using centers where members live as places of worship. Recently, Mother Moon has encouraged Unification members to establish CSW prayer halls, which function like chapels. CSW is the acronym for Cheon Shim Won, which can be translated as "the hall of the Heavenly heart." Jesus said, "God is spirit, and those who worship Him must worship Him in spirit and truth." (John 4:24) In the CSW prayer halls, the focus is on prayer and experiences with the Holy Spirit.

In 2023, Reverend Demian Dunkley, the chair and national president of FFWPU America, conducted rebirth workshops, in order to connect church members with the heart of God and of Mother Moon. Articulate and energetic, he has brought a spirit of renewal to our church communities, based on his personal relationship with Mother Moon and her messages of peace. I had a moving experience when I attended one of those workshops.

I love truth and the divine word of God, as found in the Bible and the Divine Principle. However, when I feel the spirit of God, I realize that God's love is conveyed spiritually. In order to have such spiritual experiences, it is essential that our beliefs and actions be grounded in a life of devotion and prayer.

For Mother Moon, eliminating the division of her homeland of Korea is an essential goal and gigantic undertaking. Yet she is praying and working fervently to achieve unification and to end the suffering of the Korean people, especially those who live in the North. Her strong desire is to unify the Korean people in a non-violent way and liberate the people in North Korea from communist oppression. Moreover, she is reaching out to leaders worldwide to bring hope to people who live in other communist nations that change is possible that they can be freed from the horrors of totalitarian dictatorship.

CHAPTER 41

My Alma Mater Calls

In January of 2015, the Board of Trustees of the Unification Theological Seminary asked me to become president of the seminary. That was forty years after I had been a UTS student. Nora was hesitant for me to take that position, since UTS was experiencing major legal, financial, and accreditation problems. Yet, because I love my alma mater, I accepted the challenge. I was confident that I had the knowledge and management skills that were needed to deal with a multitude of institutional, administrative, and financial problems, and I had the will power to make the changes that were necessary to save the seminary. Dr. Michael Mickler, my classmate in the first class of UTS, became Executive Vice President and was indispensable in dealing with these problems.

Prior to becoming the chief executive of UTS, the relationship between the previous president and the directors of the sponsoring church was quite contentious. Hence, I began by focusing initially on rebuilding trust with the leaders of the Family Federation for World Peace and Unification, aka, the Unification Church. I worked closely with Dr. Michael Balcomb, President of the Family Federation for World Peace and Unification in America and also Chairman of the Board of Trustees of UTS.

Also, Unification Theological Seminary was facing numerous legal, accreditation, financial, and administrative crises. My first task was to discontinue a two-year-old, undergraduate program, named Barrytown College, which had turned out to be a financial disaster. That program threatened the very existence of the seminary itself.

A major problem was that the students could not afford to pay for a private college education and received essentially full scholarships. As a result, very little income for the Barrytown College program placed a heavy financial burden on the entire institution. Indeed, the expenditures for that undergraduate program were charged to graduate program accounts and maintenance, making it appear as though Barrytown College was self-sustaining when it was not.

After extensive examination of the finances for that program and much personal soul-searching, I arranged for the Barrytown College students to do a "teach out" by transferring to other universities, including the University of Bridgeport. Closing the program was not an easy decision, since many stakeholders had invested a great deal of effort into developing that undergraduate program. They believed that a Unification education would benefit Unification-born second-generation young adults, as well as other youth. That was a very worthy goal, but the financial plan was unrealistic and not sustainable. The problem was that none of the students were able to pay the necessary tuition and room and board to sustain the program. After the undergraduate program was closed, I focused on development of the graduate programs and on creation of a new, online curriculum.

Second, due to several deficiencies, in 2014 UTS had been placed on probation by its accrediting agency, the Middle States Commission on Higher Education. My task was to reinstate full accreditation. A visiting team of educators from Middle States indicated that the UTS mission statement did not mention the relationship of the seminary with the sponsoring church and noted other issues. In response to those recommendations, the Board of Trustees approved a new mission statement that I wrote with help from some UTS administrators. In June of 2016, Middle States determined that UTS was in compliance with the accreditation standards and removed the seminary from probation.

With accreditation in place, I was ready to move on to the third issue. I had been shocked to learn that in 2014 the previous president had been notified by the US Department of Education (USDE) that the UTS application for Barrytown College students to receive financial aid had been rejected. Yet, he ignored that notice from USDE that the undergraduate students were not eligible to receive government money and arranged for them to obtain government funds through some technological glitch in the USDE website. He had not notified the UTS Board about the USDE letter.

When I arrived on the job, to my dismay I discovered that UTS was legally obligated to resolve that issue, but had neglected to do so. In fact, three days after I became President, the US Department of Education conducted an on-site program review and audit. They discovered that a total of $171,704 in student loans had been illegally awarded to the undergraduate college students. I was distraught!

It was not easy to make amends with the government, but after extensive negotiations I made an agreement with USDE for UTS to pay the reduced amount of $1,700 in restitution on the condition that the seminary abide by two mandatory requirements for the next five years: (1) UTS establish an irrevocable letter of credit, and (2) UTS be placed on heightened cash monitoring. The latter condition meant that UTS had to give loan monies to graduate students from its own funds before being reimbursed by the U.S. government. The fact that the request for recognition of the undergraduate program had been rejected by USDE had jeopardized the survival of the entire institution, including the graduate programs that had been functioning legally for more than four decades. After the seminary complied with those two requirements, the US Department of Education notified me that the case against UTS had been closed and that our status with the government had been reinstated. With that notification, I could breathe a little easier!

The fourth task concerned the cost to maintain the facilities in Barrytown. Although the Barrytown campus was in a lovely bucolic setting in New York on the Hudson River, the property was underutilized.

It cost many hundreds of thousands of dollars each year to maintain the property, especially the main building that had been built in 1929. Because the capital expenditures were exorbitant, the UTS Board decided with the approval of the leaders of the church to sell the Barrytown property and directed me to find a buyer.

We commissioned two appraisals: one indicated that the property was worth $10.1 million on the market; the other was valued at $10.3 million. Although it was difficult to find a buyer, we obtained three written bids to buy the property. The highest offer was $12 million. The Board rejected that offer, holding out for a price of $15 million. Having received no $15 million offer, the Board decided to keep the property. Four years later in June of 2023, when I was no longer either president or a trustee, a contract for the sale of the property at a price of $14 million was accepted by the Board. The closing was scheduled to take place in the fall of 2023.

Fifth, we live in a digital age. During the 1990s, Reverend Moon foresaw the value of distance learning. Since then, remote online courses have become a widespread mode of education. After an unsuccessful attempt, the seminary decided not to offer online courses, even though the necessary educational technology was available. I felt that it was now time to implement a new, online degree program that would allow our institution to offer courses to students around the globe.

With this goal in mind, UTS established a pilot, distance learning program for graduate students throughout the world using the Canvas Learning Management System. In 2019 based on the success of that program, the Middle States Commission on Higher Education and the New York State Education Department approved the UTS application for a fully online degree program. I appreciate the stakeholders who supported that initiative. It was not easy to create and implement, but it has been very successful.

A photo when I was president of UTS

Relocating the Main Campus

The days of students living and studying on faraway campuses were waning. Residential seminaries had become obsolete; many had closed. In a report to the Board, I wrote:

> *The future for UTS is in metropolitan areas where people live, work, and study and where students have easy access to classes. . . In order to prosper in this really tough time financially, UTS needs to reposition itself as an entrepreneurial, urban seminary with traditional classes and e-learning programs that rely on creative modes of delivery.*

I communicated a similar message to the stakeholders, including the alumni, that it was time to move the main campus to an urban location. I was pleased when the UTS Board passed a resolution that approved my suggestion to move the primary campus from Barrytown to New York City. Approvals from both the New York State Department of Education and the Middle States Commission on Higher Education were required. In March of 2018, I met in Philadelphia with a Middle States vice president to learn what was necessary to obtain the commission's approval to move the main campus to Manhattan, develop an online distance learning program, and close an additional learning center in Maryland. In July of 2019 both Middle States and the New York Board of Regents approved the plan to move the campus to 4 West 43rd Street in New York City.

Reverend Moon had a broad understanding of the ministry. For him, seminary graduates should go beyond the traditional role of a minister and serve people in all aspects of their lives. Indeed, many UTS graduates served as peace ambassadors in every realm of society worldwide. In September of 2015, UTS celebrated the 40th anniversary of its founding in 1975. I was very happy to help my alma mater reach that pinnacle. It validated my decision to become president.

Participating in various seminars and annual conferences of the Association of Theological Schools and the Middle States Association provided opportunities for me to promote UTS. During those sessions, I learned about the challenges and problems of other institutions. Also, I was able to share the unique vision and programs of our seminary.

Resignation as President of UTS

Being president of UTS was not easy. However, as the chief executive officer, I made the changes that were necessary to avoid several major financial crises and the possibility of closure of the institution. Satisfied that I had been able to usher the seminary successfully through many legal, accreditation, and financial crises, I resigned in August of 2019 and decided to turn the reigns of leadership over to a capable, younger educator who had the experience and skills that were required to further develop the academic programs.

I resigned as president at seventy-four years of age. I had served as the president of Unification Theological Seminary for more than four years and had achieved several major accomplishments. It was time for someone else to take the lead. I felt that the seminary needed a professional educator to expand the newly-approved distance learning program. Moreover, I believed that UTS should create a master's degree program in peace studies. Hence, it was essential that the Board choose a president who had experience with leading peace studies programs in a university.

My good friend, Dr. Thomas Ward, became my successor. By stepping aside I was able to give him an opportunity to take the lead. Dr. Ward had been a dean, vice president, and professor of peace studies at the University of Bridgeport. In 2016 I arranged for him to join the UTS Board of Directors. He helped us to develop our online, distance learning curriculum. I was confident that UTS was in good hands. Indeed, I was pleased to turn the seminary over to such a capable academic administrator.

In 2018 I discussed with the cabinet a proposal to rename our institution "Unification Peace Seminary." However, after meeting stiff resistance, I did not pursue that plan. Yet, I was happy when UTS did change its name in July of 2023 to the HJ International Graduate School for Peace and Public Leadership. That decision reflected the non-violent, peacebuilding vision and mission of our founders.

In February of 2021, I also resigned as the chairman of the Board of Directors of Bridgeport International Academy. Previously Nora had resigned as a BIA trustee. It was time for Nora and me to turn those educational responsibilities over to capable, young leaders.

CHAPTER 42

World Summit Conferences

I participated in two conferences in South Korea: the Interreligious Leadership Conference in February of 2018 and the World Summit Conference in February of 2020. It was my pleasure to join the more than two thousand dignitaries who attended a summit conference that was sponsored by the Universal Peace Federation and held at the massive Kintex Center in Seoul.

The conference included a plenary session in which Mother Moon, Ban Ki Moon (former Secretary-General of the United Nations), Newt Gingrich (former Speaker of the U.S. House of Representatives), Stephen Harper (former prime minister of Canada), and government officials from many other nations spoke. Numerous breakout sessions on timely topics provided opportunities for dialogue on contemporary issues. Attending those conferences allowed me to keep in touch with the development of God's providence and kept me informed about Mother Moon's plans.

In April of 2018 in Vienna, Austria, I participated in a conference sponsored by the Universal Peace Federation and attended Mother Moon's plenary speech. That event was based on the Unification vision for world peace and the common good. While in Austria, I visited Mauthausen, which was a notorious Nazi concentration camp during World War II. The president of the Unification Church in Korea held a ceremony in which he liberated the spirits of the people who had been imprisoned there. That experience gave me a much deeper realization of the severe, cruel, and inhumane treatment of the Jewish people during the war. In our group, there was a Jewish descendant of one of the prisoners and a German descendant of a Nazi prison guard.

My return flight on the Russian airline Aeroflot from Vienna via Moscow was problematic. On two occasions in Moscow the airplane was on the tarmac when it was forced to return to the terminal due to engine trouble. All of the passengers, including myself, had to stay overnight at the terminal before departing the next morning, which made it a long, tiring trip home. I vowed not to fly Aeroflot again!

CHAPTER 43

Florida

After five decades of total commitment to the cause, Nora and I were happy to be relieved of major administrative responsibilities, yet we remain committed to furthering God's dispensation and testifying to our founders and their world-shattering message of hope. At the same time, our desire has been to spend the latter stage of our lives with our children, their spouses, our grandchildren, and our neighbors.

Nora and I have many treasured memories. We are are grateful for having received God's blessing on our marriage, which has led to happy memories and a rewarding life. We have four delightful children who are responsible and creative. Each of them brings joy and contentment to our hearts. Also, our three grandsons are developing their own unique personalities. Experiences with all of them makes life worth living. Our lives have been based on faith in God and on love for one another, family, and friends. We are optimistic that the future will lead to a better world.

Since we have a son, daughter-in-law, and two grandsons (ages 11 and 6) who live in Florida, Nora and I decided to settle down near them in the beautiful, sunny hills of Clermont, Florida. In November of 2019, we purchased a house in the Kings Ridge Community.

Living near High's family has been wonderful. We have enjoyed spending quality time with them and helping our grandsons to build forts, do crafts, learn to swim, and enjoy life. We have accompanied them on several trips and celebrated holidays and birthdays with them.

Nora and me at our home in Florida

In 2020, two months after we moved to Florida, the Covid-19 pandemic ravished America. We felt blessed to live in a community where we could participate in many clubs and activities. The many amenities available to us include hot tubs, steam rooms, swimming pools, and two golf courses. Nora joined the quilters club and other clubs. In spite of the pandemic, we found enough activities to keep us happily occupied. I was able to play golf after having given up the sport for five decades. I made a second hole-in-one on the Kings Ridge golf course in Clermont in November of 2020.

During these latter years, we have had opportunities to reflect on our lives and write our recollections of what we experienced during the last fifty-plus years in our church movement.

In our community of 2,000 homes, we found many friends among the senior citizens living here and have expanded our outreach to a wide circle of acquaintances. Some of our neighbors have read Nora's memoir titled, *Spiritual Connections: Living in the Flow of God's Love*, which explains her unique and amazing life story. We hope we have been a blessing to them and others in our retirement community.

Nora was raised on a Mennonite family farm. As a female leader, she traveled the globe with celebrities and public officials. Her life of faith is extraordinary, and she has had an amazing career. Her other book *Circles of Angels: How You Can Call Your Own Circle of Angels to Energize Your Life* is a practical guide on how to obtain help from the angelic world in every aspect of one's life. Many neighbors and friends have come to know the story of her life through reading those two books.

Florida is a beautiful state with a pleasant climate year-round. We enjoy living here. Sometimes we marvel that our residential community feels like paradise. Some of our neighbors call it "God's waiting room." With a somewhat more relaxed schedule, we have joined a writer's club and had time to write our autobiographies and reflect on how we have lived our lives.

On October 21, 2020, after fifty years of marriage, Nora and I celebrated our golden wedding anniversary. However, due to the Covid-19 pandemic, our plan to celebrate by taking a cruise with High's family was delayed. Later in April of 2022, we went with them on a cruise to Mexico and Honduras.

The pandemic had some impact on our lives; however, through online programs, such as sermons, meetings, webinars, and rallies, we have been able to keep informed and remain involved in developments within our movement. The Unification Church, recently designated *Heavenly Parents' Holy Community* by Mother Moon, creatively held online "Rallies of Hope" in which she, heads of state, and other dignitaries spoke. I like that description of the church, although it is not the official name. It indicates the inclusiveness of our movement and reflects the overall purpose of this movement to embrace all people and create a world of love, peace, and goodness centered on God.

A major event was the virtual "Peace Starts with Me Rally" in August of 2020 at which Mother Moon and also Bishop Noel Jones, pastor of the City of Refuge Church in Los Angeles, spoke. We have been able to view online the celebration of many holy days and events, consequently keeping in touch through those virtual programs. Webinars and Zoom calls became a way of life. Through sophisticated technology, the international movement allowed us to participate in programs and events sponsored by the Universal Peace Federation and *The Washington Times*, keeping us informed about activities everywhere.

CHAPTER 44

Global Citizenship

In these pages, I have sought to explain some of the reasons why I believe Drs. Sun Myung and Hak Ja Han Moon are a messianic couple. I call them my spiritual parents. Indeed, they are the luminaries for all of humanity at this watershed moment in human history. For me, that is an article of faith.

Even though Nora and I have faced struggles and confronted quagmires during our lives, we are grateful to God and our church movement for providing opportunities to live meaningful lives. We were fortunate to be at the right place at the right time. Having met Father and Mother Moon when we were young, we were able to participate in this historic providence when God's messengers walked the earth, and we experienced astonishing adventures with both of them.

In October of 2020, Mother Moon recognized Nora and I as a Cheonbo couple or a "heavenly treasure," and as citizens of Cheon Il Guk or "God's Kingdom of Eternal Peace," which translated literally means citizens of "the nation of cosmic peace and harmony."

Nora and I (and many members of the Unification Church) have become global citizens! We have traveled around the world and made countless life-long friendships with many people. We have been able to help them to understand God's plan to realize one global family for people of all races, cultures, nationalities, and religious creeds. Our lives have been happy, rich, and fulfilling. We have had a marriage that has been a lifelong commitment of love, respect, and excitement centered on our Heavenly Parent. We are optimistic about God's plan for the future and are thankful that we have been able to contribute to world peace.

We have been blessed with four wonderful children who bring joy to us as we observe them having become mature. Intelligent, creative, artistic, and talented—each of them brings happiness to our hearts. Our three grandsons are developing their own unique personalities. Interacting with them has enriched our lives greatly.

Living near High and his family in the sunshine state has been wonderful. We are discovering God's presence by hosting relatives and friends and most importantly spending time with our children and grandchildren. All of our children and grandchildren have visited us in Florida and were able to enjoy this splendid vacation spot. Those get-togethers are times of sharing and keeping up with one another's lives.

Our three grandsons, Ari in Seattle and Brayden and Jaxon in Florida, have had opportunities to deepen their relationships. Recently, while we were visiting High's home, Brayden excitedly rushed into the room with his iPad saying, "I was playing a game and suddenly my cousin, Ari, came on and was playing also." His eyes sparkled with enthusiasm. Moments like that are precious.

I believe that God had a plan for my life that led me from Indiana to Washington DC. Due to the career choices I made while I was in high school and college, I moved to the nation's capital as a young man and met the Unification Church.

Now, I realize that good things happened in my life when I had the courage to take a leap of faith into the unknown. The decision I made fifty-five years ago enabled me to live an amazing, purpose-filled life. Moving ever onward and upward in a life that has been rich in the ever-flowing love of God, I have shared this incredible journey with my extraordinary wife, Nora, and precious friends and family members.

CHAPTER 45

Into the Future

The Evolution of God's Providence

The world is in the midst of a transition from an old to a new era. Everything is changing. Some individuals may fear new ideas, leaders, and movements, in part because they lack the confidence to take risks. Change involves taking chances—venturing into the unknown. Most people are comfortable with the status quo. Yet when old patterns and institutions disappear, uncertainty occurs. Reverend and Mrs. Moon predicted that in the future humanity will experience an evolutionary process in which people will have greater interest in God and that which is moral and spiritual.

Personal Observations

Personally, I have observed the creativity of our founders and the innovations that they proposed. Sometimes employees in other organizations who advocate major reforms are pushed to the periphery and ignored. In contrast, both Drs. Sun Myung and Hak Ja Han Moon have advocated major changes for the church and its members. Those reforms are a reflection of the development of God's providence progressing over time toward the ultimate goal of establishing the kingdom of God on earth, i.e., "a new heaven and a new earth." (Rev. 21:1)

Around the breakfast table, Reverend Moon spoke impromptu—usually in the Korean language. His comments were inspiring and stimulating. Unfortunately, they were not recorded. Sometimes Father Moon met with dignitaries and guests. On most occasions, he interacted privately with his closest disciples—frequently discussing new proposals with them before those plans were announced publicly.

Since we never knew what Reverend Moon might say at the breakfast table, we needed to be ready to respond if asked to do so. Spontaneously sometimes he announced leadership changes, asking someone to assume a new role or announcing a new organization or project. At other times, leaders were demoted. Sometimes that same person later was given a new role, which I experienced. For me, that meant the end of one cycle and the beginning of a new one. It was all part of a personal journey through life, which included many "ups and downs" that were followed often by a rise to a new level of maturity, responsibility, and happiness.

I have observed that Mother Moon's leadership style is very similar to that of her late husband. She is spontaneous, creative, and very decisive. She is a bold leader who does not hesitate to declare publicly what she believes to be the will of God, including explaining her providential mission to the general public.

Change is a deviation from the status quo. It consists of taking chances and "stepping out on a limb." Taking risks is essential to the process of becoming a responsible and mature adult. Our loving God continues to present each person with opportunities to grow, as human civilization progresses toward His ultimate goal to establish the kingdom of heaven on earth.

Addendum

The Papers and Documents of Hugh and Nora Spurgin are in storage. Included among them are historical documents, photos signed by Reverend Moon, and a detailed chronology of Nora and Hugh's lives.

In addition to studying the life and teachings of Jesus and Moses, Hugh was intrigued by the lives and writings of many profound thinkers, including: John Calvin, Roger Williams, John Locke, George Whitefield, Jonathan Edwards, Benjamin Franklin, Ralph Waldo Emerson, Pearl S. Buck, Albert Einstein, Immanuel Kant, Albrecht Ritschl, Eleanor Roosevelt, Jane Austen, Mark Twain, Harriet Beecher Stowe, Milton Freidman, Charles Grandison Finney, Theodore Weld, Karl Marx, Max Weber, Charles H. Spurgeon, Walter Rauschenbusch, Leo Tolstoy. Albert Schweitzer, Aleksandr Solzhenitsyn, Arnold Toynbee, Mahatma Gandhi, Alexis de Tocqueville and Martin Luther King, Jr.

About the Author

Born in Roswell New Mexico and raised in Terre Haute Indiana, Hugh Spurgin is a graduate of Indiana State University. He received a masters degree in public administration from Syracuse University and a masters degree in divinity from Union Theological Seminary, then went on to earn a Ph.D. in American history from Columbia University.

Dr. Spurgin has had a 55-year career in management and leadership roles in various non-profit religious and educational organizations, serving as president of Unification Theological Seminary, vice-president of the Family Federation for World Peace and Unification, president of Bridgeport International Academy, and executive director of the International Cultural Foundation and Professors World Peace Academy. His efforts to promote peace among people of very diverse backgrounds took him throughout America and to many nations throughout the world.

Hugh is known in ecumenical circles as a dependable leader and person of integrity who has sought to communicate an understanding of the providence of God to his contemporaries. He has shared his life for 53 years with his wife Nora. In 1970 they were married in South Korea in a Unification ceremony consisting of 777 couples. They have raised four remarkable children—all of whom are married and have professional careers. They have three talented grandsons.

In *Passion and Grit*, the author delineates his profound spiritual and intellectual experiences. Hugh believes he was led by God from his hometown in Indiana to Washington, DC where in 1968 he met members of the Unification Church movement, which was founded by Reverend Moon, a charismatic religious leader from Korea. That unforeseen encounter had a major impact on his life and was the impetus for his passion and quest to bring about a peaceful world, a mission to which he dedicated his life.